BOLLAND AND THE HODDER VALLEY

A History

Margaret Greenwood
and
Father Charles Bolton

Landy Publishing
2000

This is a photographic reprint of the original edition, which was privately published in 1955. To it have been added the illustrations, a new introduction by Chris Spencer, a list of further reading by Robin Greenwood and a names index by Crispin Edwards of the Slaidburn Heritage Centre.

 The photographs have been loaned from the collection of the Slaidburn Heritage Centre, and the publishers wish to specially thank Allan Wood, Margaret Brenchley, Pye's of Clitheroe and Miss M. N. Gaskins for permission to use their photographs.

ISBN 1 872895 50 6

British Library in Cataloguing Publication Data.
A catalogue record of this book is available from the British Library.

Layout by Mike Clarke: 01254 395848
Printed by Nayler the Printer Ltd., Accrington: 01254 234247

INTRODUCTION

I am delighted to have been invited to write a new introduction for the re-print of this book. I first came across a copy of Greenwood and Bolton's '*Bolland Forest and the Hodder Valley*' some fifteen years ago in Whalley Library, ('Bolland' being the ancient spelling of the modern 'Bowland'). I had not previously known about it, although I had been researching the area for some time. I was fascinated by its contents.

It was clear to me that this was the book I had long wished existed but had never believed that it did. As I turned the pages, I was engrossed with the contents: Colonel Parker's short history; Tudor feuds on Croasdale; lists of farmers, and so on – and many of the old Bolland names which were familiar to me littered the pages.

Today, as we start a new Millennium, the book still has a great appeal to me. It contains a wealth of information for anyone interested in the history of the Bolland area, and makes reference to so many sources (unfortunately not always quoted!) of original documents, many of which are deposited in the Lancashire Record Office, Preston, the Borthwick Institute, York and the Public Record Office, Kew.

After the book's publication in 1955, there was little else written on the area for some time. Then in 1973, John Porter produced his PhD thesis '*The Reclamation and Settlement of Bowland 1500-1650*' which used the court rolls of the Manor of Slaidburn as its primary source. This work has since been carried on by Professor Richard Hoyle of the University of Central Lancashire and it is hoped that he will publish his findings soon. Reg Postlethwaite and I have published the '*Parish Registers of Slaidburn 1600-1837/52*', and I am currently working on producing transcripts of the court rolls of the Manor of Slaidburn along with other material. Dr Craig Thornber has recently published the registers of several non-conformist chapels in the area and has now turned his attention to the parish registers of Mitton. The Chipping Local History Society is about to publish another diary for the period 1733-34 of the Reverend Peter Walkden who ministered at both the Newton and Hesketh Lane chapels.

One might therefore say that Greenwood and Bolton's book has been, and still is, an inspiration to local and family historians of the area. As is stated in their introduction, no history is ever complete due to the vast wealth of material available, but the last fifty years or so have gone a long way to rectifying a dearth of published history of the area.

However, there is much still to do, with, for example, a mass of information in the Duchy of Lancaster archives at the Public Record Office concerning pleas and depositions, and the court rolls of the Manor of Slaidburn going back to 1519 in an almost continuous sequence. The estate papers, deeds, etc. of the King-Wilkinson family, who at one time owned many properties in the Slaidburn area, have recently been made available to the public in the Lancashire Record Office, but the collection is not yet properly catalogued. Some primary sources have unfortunately disappeared – the note book of Thomas Oakes Wright who owned the Harrop Hall estate in the early 1800's, and quoted in this book, was not found amongst the rest of the estate papers at the Wrexham solicitors' office last year when visited by Professor Richard Hoyle and Dr Henry French.

Margaret Greenwood (nee Longworth) (1888-1969) of Clerk Hill, Whalley, often went on long excursions in the Forest of Bolland with Father Charles Anselm Bolton (1905-1970), a native of Longridge and parish priest of St. Mary's, Clayton-le-Moors in the early 1950s. Their love of the rural scenery and the remote, peaceful environment, which still exists today, comes across vividly in their book

Thanks are due to Robin Greenwood and his cousins for granting permission to use their grandmother's writing, and to Robin for compiling 'Suggested Further Reading'; also to Crispin Edwards for the enthusiasm he has put into the project; in particular finding photographs which have been added to the Slaidburn Heritage Centre's archive and used in this re-print, and for compiling the index.

One day, an author may produce a new history of Bolland, but until that day, Greenwood and Bolton's '*Bolland Forest and the Hodder Valley*' will remain **the** authority on the history of the area. The book is a lasting monument to them and should serve as an invitation to visit an area of great natural beauty, straddling both Yorkshire and Lancashire.

Chris Spencer
Preston, June 2000

SUGGESTED FURTHER READING

Ackerly, Rev. F. G. ***History of Mitton*** (1947)

Best, D. ***A short history of Clitheroe in Lancashire*** (1988)

Brazendale, D. ***Lancashire's Historic Halls*** (1994)

Cunliffe-Shaw, R. ***The Royal Forests of Lancaster*** (1956)

Farrer, W. (Editor) ***Court Rolls of Honour of Clitheroe***, 3 Vols. (1897)

Farrer, W. (Editor) Some Court Rolls, etc. of Thomas, Earl of Lancaster, **Record Soc. of Lancs. & Ches.**, Vol.41 (1901)

Farrer, W. & Brownhill, J. (Editors) ***The Victoria History of the County of Lancaster***, Vols. 2, 6 & 7 (1908, 1911 & 1912)

Faull, M. L. & Moorhouse, S. A. (Editors) ***West Yorkshire: An Archaeological Survey to AD 1500***, 4 Vols. (1981)

Fishwick, H. *Pleadings and Depositions in the Duchy Court of Lancaster*, **Record Soc. of Lancs. & Ches.**, Vol.40 (1899)

French, H. R. & Hoyle, R. W. *The Land Market of a Pennine Manor : Slaidburn 1650-1780*, **Continuity & Change**, Vol. 14 (1999)

Gregson, M. ***Portfolio of Fragments – Lancashire***, 3rd edition (1869)

Ironfield, C. The Parish of Chipping During the 17th Century, **Trans. of the Hist. Soc. of Lancs. and Ches.**, Vol. 127 (1978)

Jenet, S. ***Deserts of England*** (1964)

Lancaster, W. T. & Baildon, ***W. P. Coucher Book of Kirkstall Abbey*** (1904)

Lofthouse, J. ***Lancashire's Old Families*** (1972)

Manning, R. B. ***Hunters and Poachers: A Cultural and Social History of Unlawful Hunting in England 1485-1640*** (1993)

Mitchell, W. R. ***Bowland and Pendle Hill*** (1971)

Musson, R. C. *A Bronze Age Cave Site in the Little Bolland Area*, **Trans. of the Lancs. & Ches. Antiquarian Soc.** (1947)

Peel, A. ***The Manor of Knowlmere – Its History and Owners*** (1913)

Peel, A. ***A Short History of the Parish of Slaidburn*** (1922)

Porter, J. *The Reclamation and Settlement of Bowland, with special reference to the period 1500-1650*, unpublished Ph.D. Thesis, **University of London** (1973)

Porter, J. A *Forest in Transition: Bowland 1500-1650*, **Trans. of the Historic Soc. of Lancs. and Ches.**, Vol.125 (1975)

Porter, J. *Waste Land Reclamation in the 16th and 17th Centuries*, **Trans. of the Historic Soc. of Lancs. and Ches.**, Vol. 127 (1978)

Porter, J. ***The Forest of Bowland – Its Landscape and History*** (1994)

Smith, T. C. ***History of Chipping*** (1893)

Somerville, R. ***The History of the Duchy of Lancaster***, 2 Vols. (1953 & 1970)

Spencer, C. J. & Postlethwaite, R. H. ***The Registers of Saint Andrew's Parish Church, Slaidburn 1600-1837/52***, 2 Vols. (1994 & 1998)

Spencer, C. J. ***Parish of Slaidburn, 1841 Census*** (1999); ***Slaidburn & Bowland Will Index 1389-1688*** (1999); ***The Court Rolls of the Manor of Slaidburn 1724-1733***, Vol.1 (2000); ***Slaidburn and Bowland Wills & Administration***, Vols. 1 & 2 (2000), Privately published by C. J. Spencer, 17 Black Bull Lane, Fulwood, Preston, PR2 3PT

Swinglehurst, A. N. ***The Swinglehursts of Bowland*** (1991)

Thornber, Dr. C.W. ***The Registers of Holden Chapel 1771-1897-1908*** (1997) Privately published by Dr. Thornber

Weld, J. ***History of Leagram*** (1913)

Whitaker, The Rev. T. D. ***History of the Ancient Parish of Whalley and Honour of Clitheroe***, 4th edition, 2 Vols. (1872).

Whitaker, The Rev. T. D. ***The History and Antiquities of the Deanery of Craven in the County of York***, 3rd edition (1879)

Wood, P. N. *On the Little British Kingdom of Craven*, **Northern History**, Vol. 32 (1996)

Young, C. R. ***The Royal Forests of Medieval England*** (1979)

Local lads and lasses engage in the country dances of old England outside the **Hark to Bounty** in the late 1940s. The Court Room steps provide a fine vantage point. The photographer was probably in an upstairs room of the Youth Hostel. At the top of the photograph, a Hodder Motor Services 'bus is parked against the pinfold.

Huntingdon House, originally two houses, provides the background and Slaidburn Cenotaph the centre-piece for this view of the arrival of the May Queen, Lois Worswick, about 1950. The Slaidburn Band have left their uniforms at home. A delightful village community scene viewed by a lad whose father had a motor car with a sliding sun-roof.

CONTENTS.

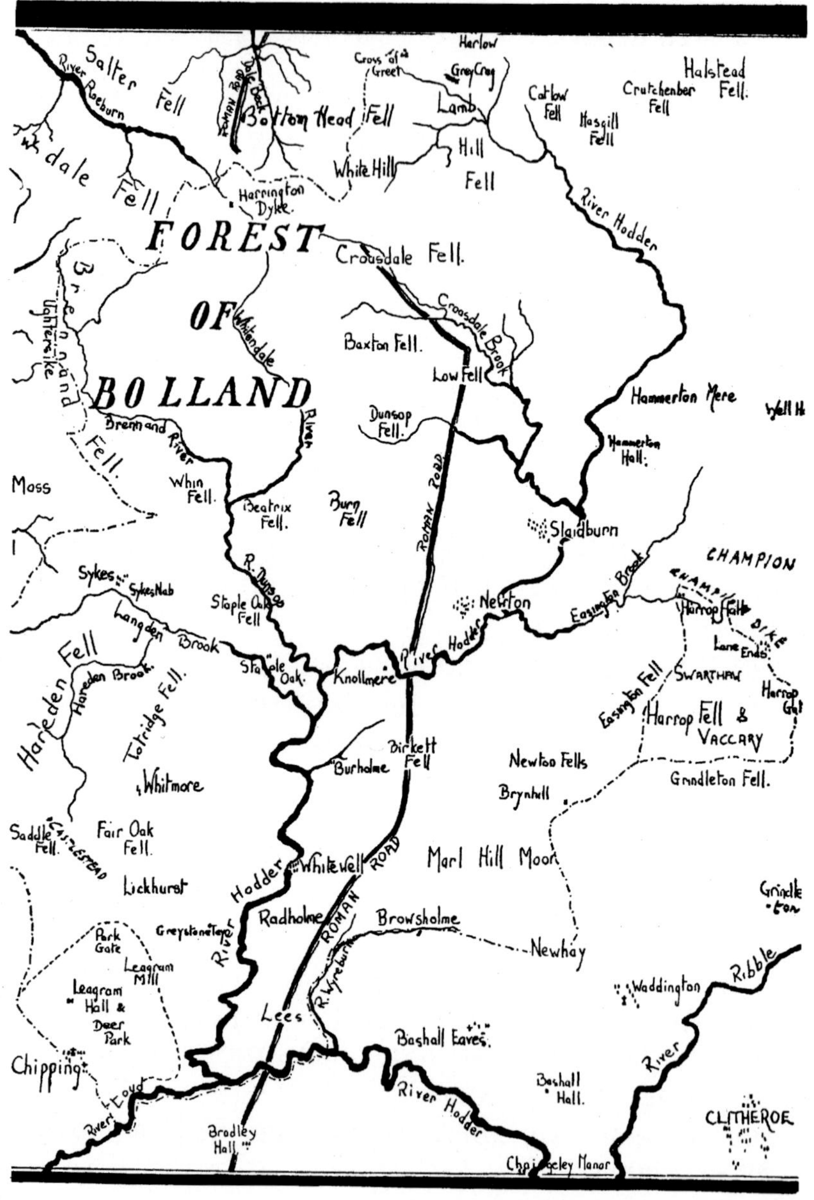
Salter Fell
River Roeburn
Harlow
Cross of Greet
Grey Crag
Halstead Fell
Crutchenber Fell
Catlow Fell
Hasgill Fell
Roman Road
Dale Beck
Bottom Head Fell
Lamb
Hill
Fell
White Hill
Harrington Dyke
FOREST
OF
BOLLAND
Croasdale Fell
River Hodder
Whitendale
Croasdale Brook
Baxton Fell
Low Fell
River
Hammerton Mere
Dunsop Fell
Hammerton Hall
Brennand Fell
Brennand River
Whin Fell
Moss
Beatrix Fell
Burn Fell
Roman Road
Slaidburn
CHAMPION
Sykes
Sykes Nab
R. Dunsop
Staple Oak Fell
Newton
Easington Brook
Harrop Hall
Langden Brook
Lane Ends
Staple Oak
Knollmere
River Hodder
Hareden Brook
Swarthaw
Easington Fell
Harrop Fell &
Vaccary
Totridge Fell
Hareden Fell
Birkett Fell
Burholme
Newton Fells
Grindleton Fell
Whitmore
Brynhull
Saddle Fell
Fair Oak Fell
Hodder
Whitewell
Roman Road
Marl Hill Moor
Lickhurst
Radholme
Browsholme
Park Gate
Leagram Mill
River
Newhay
Leagram Hall &
Deer Park
R. Wyreburn
Lees
Waddington
Ribble
Bashall Eaves
Chipping
River
Bashall Hall
River Loud
River Hodder
CLITHEROE
Bradley Hall
Chaigeley Manor

FOREWORD.

No history yet written can claim to tell all that could be told about the past, and this history of Bolland would never have been published if the authors had thought that it must be complete in order to be worth while. In order to make this book, much material has been discarded as unimportant, and some material—notably the history of Slaidburn—has been set aside in order to make the book more manageable.

Several areas were at an early date part of Bolland ; at an early date they became independent, although by their situation they continued to be closely connected with the Forest. Such were Grindleton, West Bradford, Waddington, Mitton, Bashall, Slaidburn, Easington, Hamerton, and Newton. No history of Bolland could fail to contact these districts and their inhabitants in various ways, yet because at an early date they were separated from what was truly the Forest of Bolland their story is in some ways independent. For the sake of concentrating on the Forest story a good deal of the local history of these districts has been omitted. Moreover some of that history has already been printed in a *History of Slaidburn* and a *History of Mitton*, not to mention the earlier accounts in Whitaker's great folios about Whalley.[1]

Yet in spite of omissions, deliberate or otherwise, there is much in these pages about places like Slaidburn, and about Slaidburn families. One of the features of the present work is that it tries to tell something about the ordinary dwellers in Bolland—the sheep and cattle-raising farmers, the craftsmen, the keepers of the deer, the makers of fences and ditches, and all manner of labouring folk.

The Forest, because it was a royal estate, probably suffered from the human point of view by the fact that so much of it was preserved as the haunt of red and fallow deer or as a source of timber. As regards both the deer and the timber very little was done by royal command to increase this inheritance or to exploit it ; it was considered sufficient to let nature produce with the help of a few keepers to drive off intruders in search of either the deer or the timber. In fact, towards the end of the Middle Ages, we find that nature was not responding well enough either with the deer or the forest trees to resist the encroachments of the humans who claimed spoils, sometimes by royal licence but very often without licence. The dwellers in the Forest helped themselves when they could—and that was often—and the dwellers outside the Forest, chiefly the nearby squires and their men, looked upon

[1] Miss A. Peel's *History of Slaidburn* and the *History of Mitton* by the Rev. F. G. Ackerley.

the royal preserve of the Forest as a happy hunting ground that was theirs because the King never came hunting there.

When in the reign of Mary Tudor the Forest of Little Bolland ceased to be a deer-park, it was already becoming farm-land, and the same is true of Great Bolland when it was given in 1662 to be part of the estate of George Monk, Duke of Albemarle, one of the most remarkable figures of English history, and who well deserved the reward that a grateful monarch, Charles II, bestowed upon him for bringing him back to England. Bolland should be proud that it was associated with so great a man at such an important moment of England's history.

To avoid further explanation, it should be said that Little Bolland is the Lancashire side of the Forest, and that Great Bolland is the Yorkshire side. Most of the history is naturally concerned with Great Bolland, although the Lancashire side is not neglected.[1]

There are several sources of Bolland history that are to a great extent still unrevealed, for example the Slaidburn parish register and the numerous rolls and volumes of the ancient Slaidburn Court, at present in Clitheroe Castle. It has not been possible to explore these fully. The amount of historical material available presents a problem to the historian who insists on complete thoroughness in his survey. No doubt it was partly due to the mass of material that the late Colonel J. Parker of Browsholme never finished his projected history of Bolland. The present study owes much to his notes and to his pioneer work, as a tribute to which Colonel Parker's short history of Bolland has been reprinted here. It will serve to give the reader a good general introduction to the Bolland story. His short but masterly survey will help to make up for what the present work omits, especially concerning such places as Bashall and Mitton.

The reader who is interested in the old places of Bolland, the old landmarks, the old names, the old families, the old way of life, and half-forgotten memories, will find much to study in these pages. He will not find a continuous story but a series of pictures rather like those in an old family album, each one telling part of a story and being vaguely linked with some of the others. Such is our history of Bolland, and we commend it to the kind judgement and consideration of all those who know Bolland and its people.

[1] J. Weld's *History of Leagram*, Chetham Society, 1913, is useful and supplementary information is in Tom C. Smith's *History of Chipping*, Preston, 1893, for Little Bolland.

CHAPTER I.

BOLLAND.

By COLONEL J. PARKER, C.B., F.S.A., of Browsholme.
(Read before the "Society of Genealogists," 5, Bloomsbury-square, London, 11th February, 1926.)

I. – Geography.

Bolland is a wild mountainous tract in the West Riding of the County of York which here juts out into Lancashire, by which it is encompassed on three sides.

It is bounded on the N.W. by the watershed that divides it from Hornby and the Forests of Lancaster and Bleasdale : on the S.W. by Chippingdale and the River Hodder : on the S.E. by the River Ribble : and on the N.E. by Bolton, Gisburn and Gisburn Forest in Yorkshire, part of the great Percy fee, from which it is separated by a series of brooks and dykes.

At the eastern corner lies the Cistercian Abbey of Salley : just below the southern point is Whalley Abbey, the latest Cistercian foundation in England : about half-way between them, under the shadow of Pendle hill, lies Clitheroe Castle – the "caput" of the Honor.

The River Hodder, which rises near Bolland Knots to the north, runs across Bolland, dividing it almost in half, to Whitewell whence it forms the S.E. boundary.

The area is about 140 square miles.

The district is surveyed in Domesday under the Manor of Grindleton. "In Gretlintone," we are told, "Earl Tosti had a Manor." It was at that time, with Amounderness and other of the Earl's Lancashire estates, in the hands of Count Roger of Poitou.

The Manor comprised the following vills or townships : Grindleton, Bradford, Waddington, Bashall, Mitton, Hamerton, Slaidburn, Battersby, Newton, Bogewurth, Easington, Radom and Sotleie.

In all, there were 38 carucates of land : two centuries later these 38 had dwindled to 20. At the present time there is practically no land ploughed in the whole area.

Early in the 12th century, Chippingdale was added to Bolland. It is in Lancashire and is now called Little Bolland – 7 square miles in area. When describing the Yorkshire Forests in the "Victoria County History," Dr. Cox omitted all mention of Bolland. I wrote to the Editor asking the reason. Is it possible,

I asked, that the learned writer supposes that Bolland is in Lancashire? In reply, Dr. Cox admitted that he had been under that delusion : but, while apologising, he wished to point out to me that by far the greater part of Bolland is in Lancashire – 7 out of 150 square miles !

II. – Name.

A word as to the name. It has always been pronounced Bolland by the older inhabitants. Outsiders call and spell it Bowland, from a silly notion (encouraged by Dr. Whitaker) that it was a land of Bows and Arrows. The earliest spelling is Boeland, and we then have Boghe, Bou, Bov, Bowe-land. Dr. Ekwall suggests Boghe – a bend : and refers to a bend in the River Ribble, outside the area, as the possible origin. But I know of no such bend. There is a much simpler solution. This was essentially a cattle-raising district. The whole Forest was parcelled out into vaccaries or cattle-rearing farms and, over such portions as could not so be dealt with, the farmers had "beast-gates" allotted to them. Bolland was and is the land of cattle – from the Old Norse Bu = cattle, Bol = a byre or shippon.

III. – Churches.

As to Churches ; Bolland contained the Parish of Slaidburn and part of the Parish of Mitton – the rest of which was in Lancashire. The remainder of Bolland (the Forest) was attached to the Chapel of S. Michael in Clitheroe Castle. When, in the 14th century, that Chapel ceased to exist, the Forest became in fact extra-parochial. The little Chapel attached to the Manor Court at Whitewell was served occasionally by a Priest from Clitheroe Parish Church, where the inhabitants of the Forest had rights of marriage and burial. At later dates Waddington – which acquired a semi-parochial status in 1443 – and Grindleton were carved out of Mitton : Dale Head out of Slaidburn : and Whitewell was constituted a Parish. Only Browsholme now remains extra-parochial.

IV. – Lords.

We have seen that at the time of the Domesday Survey this district was held by Roger of Poitou. But he, adhering to Duke Robert of Normandy, who invaded England in August, 1101, was banished and his estates were forfeited. They were granted, for the most part, to Robert de Lascy, whose powerful interests King Henry was anxious to win over. The original grants have perished: but there are Memoranda at the Record Office of three which concern our subject :–

1. A grant of Chippingdale, Aighton, Bailey, Dutton and other lands in Lancashire, to Robert de Lascy.

2. A grant to him of Bolland – which Robert formerly held under Roger the Poictevin.

3. An undertaking by the King that the lands granted to Robert de Lascy should be no more in the Forest than they were at the date of the grant.

But Robert de Lascy, like the Poictevin, went over to the King's enemies and, in 1114, all his lands were forfeited and bestowed upon Hugh de la Val. On the death of Hugh, quickly followed by the murder of his successor, Ilbert de Lascy – son of Robert – was restored to all the possessions of his father in 1135. With the descendants of Ilbert de Lascy they remained, passing to the House of Lancaster and so to the Crown on the accession of Henry IV. At the Restoration, in 1660, the Honor of Clitheroe – which included Bolland – was granted to Monk, Duke of Albemarle ; whose representative, 80 years ago, sold the Yorkshire part of the Honor – i.e., Bolland and the Manor of Slaidburn—to Colonel Charles Towneley of Towneley, whose nieces are now owners of the Manor and such portions of the land as remain unsold. Ever since the 14th century there have been constant purchases by the occupiers, both of land and forestal rights—not to mention the earlier grants of which I shall now treat.

The freehold estates acquired under these early grants from the de Lascys were styled Manors or reputed Manors or Lordships and constituted the Liberties of Bolland, as distinguished from the Forest. Their owners did homage at the Chief Court of Bolland, held at Slaidburn, and were the Judicators or Assessors at that Court.

V. – Mitton.

We have seen that in the Autumn of 1101 the King granted to Robert de Lascy Bolland and adjacent estates. Robert, by his charter dated 23rd November, 1102 (an interesting early date) gave to Ralph le Rous – Red Ralph – Great Mitton in Bolland together with Aighton, Bailey and other lands in Lancashire. This gift was confirmed by Ilbert de Lascy, son of Robert, by a charter in which he describes Ralph le Rous as his brother. Ralph was the ancester of the Mitton family and probably built the Church there, of which he, his son and his grandson, were successively Parsons or Rectors. About 1220 the Advowson was granted by Robert of Mitton to Cockersand Abbey – a gift that, after some litigation, was confirmed in 1236 by Ralph of Mitton, son of Robert.

In Kirkby's "Inquest" – 1284 – Mitton-cum-Withgill is returned as held by this Ralph under the Earl of Lincoln. Ralph granted it to Thomas le Surreys or Sotheron who in 1312 settled the Manor of Mitton by Fine on himself for life with remainder to his sons Thomas and Adam and their heirs in tail. The Sotherons were non-resident, having large estates elsewhere, and moved into Shropshire early in the 16th century. The Manor passed through various hands and is now owned by Major Aspinall, of Standen, near Clitheroe.

On behalf of Major Aspinall, there is – or rather has been – yearly held the Court Leet, Court Baron and View of Frank Pledge of the Manor of Mitton-with-Crook. Major Aspinall also holds the Advowson. This, on the dissolution of Cockersand Abbey, was acquired by the Shireburnes of Stonyhurst – the direct male descendants of Red Ralph, the grantee of 1102. The Shireburne Chapel in Mitton Church contains some fine late effigies of members of this family : the last of whom, the Duchess of Norfolk, dying without issue, the estates passed to the Welds of Lulworth. In 1792, when the Jesuits were driven from St. Omer, Mr. Weld handed over Stonyhurst to that Order, under whose care it has developed into a great College.

The family of Colthurst owned a considerable estate in Mitton near Edisford early in the 15th century. The main line merged into heirs female in Elizabethan times, having sent out thriving branches to Gargrave, Somersetshire and Ireland. The bridge over the Ribble, rebuilt in 1341, is now happily scheduled under the Ancient Monuments Act. At Edisford also – but in Lancashire – was a Hospital of St. Nicholas for Lepers.

VI. – Withgill.

At what date and in what manner Withgill alias Crook became separated from Great Mitton cannot be definitely stated. It was most probably the marriage portion of Maud wife of Adam of Bury who joined with her husband in 1226 in levying a Fine as to eight bovates of land in Withgill to be held of them and the heirs of Maud. In 1258, on the death of Edmund de Lascy, it was found that :–

> "Adam of Bury holds 40 acres of land in Old Withgill and pays 4s. yearly for everything."

In 1305 there was a Fine levied between Henry of Bury and Edmund Talbot as to the bounds between Withgill and Bashall. The Poll Tax return for 1379 shows another Henry of Bury at Withgill and his heiress carried the Manor to the Singletons in marriage.

The Singletons were a somewhat lawless clan. in 1394 William Singleton of Withgill was indicted for killing one of the King's Justices and outlawed. There was strife between them and their neighbour Talbot of Bashall. The Plea Rolls record an attack on Bashall Hall in 1461 by the Singletons and their friends, over 100 in all ; and soon afterwards, at an Inquest before the Coroner upon the body of Alice Singleton, gentlewoman, it was presented that John Talbot son of Margaret Colthurst of Bashall, gentleman, on the 12th January, 1469, at Mitton, of great malice long thought out, struck the said Alice in the breast with a lance, price sixpence, and gave her a mortal blow and she instantly died. And Richard Talbot of Bashall, gentleman, struck her with an arrow and gave her a mortal blow in the lower part of the head, as far as the brain : and Thrustan Waddington, of Wyghton, co. York, yoman, struck her with a stick called a longdebeve on the right side of her belly which would have killed her but that she was already dead. And Thomas Talbot, of Bashall, Esquire, Nicholas Tempest, of Brayswell, gentleman, and others—a long list, filling two membranes of the Roll—were present and abetted. They—being good Yorkists—produced the King's pardon.

Alan Singleton, the last of Withgill, died in 1503, leaving a daughter Ann who married Sir William Leyland, of Morleys, Lancashire. Through a Leyland heiress Withgill passed to the Tyldesleys and was forfeited in 1715 when Mr. Tyldesley joined the Rebels and was captured at Preston.

Among the Forfeited Estate Papers at the Record Office is an interesting Deposition by Thomas Rishton, of Greengore (near Stonyhurst), gentleman : who states that Edward Tildesley—grandfather of Mr. Tildesley taken among the Rebels at Preston—was, about the year 1661, seised in fee of an estate called Crook in the parish of Mitton, Yorkshire—that he went to Portugal with the English Ambassador who was sent to bring over the Infanta of Portugal, afterwards Queen Catherine, wife of King Charles II.—that he courted a Portuguese lady, one of her attendants, and got her with child—that this lost him (who was a married man) all the Court favour : and for this (being a Papist) he was enjoined, by way of penance, to give the lady £1,200 to £1,500 as compensation. To raise this sum he mortgaged the Crook estate of about £200 per annum to English Popish Priests or to some persons in trust for them : and the lady, for her penance, was enjoined to give the money to the Priests, which she did.

Evidence of the way in which this money was raised exists in the form of a lease, dated 5th November, 1667 ; by which, in consideration of £86.13s.4d., Edward Tildesley demised to William Cowell, of Crook, yeoman, a messuage in Crook for a term of 190 years from the death of the then tenant at a peppercorn rent. William Cowell's daughter married Edmund Sagar. The farm has long been known as Sagar Fold and is still in possession of the family, who bought the freehold some 40 years ago, before the expiration of their lease.

VII.—Waddington.

In 1267, Roger Tempest of Bracewell occurs on the Assize Rolls as Lord of Waddington. How he acquired this Manor is not proved, as no Charter has yet been traced.

According to the Elizabethan Heralds, Roger obtained it by marriage with Alice, daughter and heir of Sir Walter of Waddington. Alice may have been a daughter of Sir Walter but she was most certainly not his heir, for he had at least five sons who left issue : and there is nothing to show that the Waddington family ever held the Manor. Another point is that Alice had her dower assessed out of Waddington, which would be strange if it had belonged to her. It is much more probable that there was a direct grant to the Tempests from de Lascy.

I need hardly repeat the well-known story of the betrayal of King Henry VI., who while dining at Waddington Hall was betrayed by the Talbots. Escaping through a window he fled towards Clitheroe, over the hipping stones at Brungerley, but was captured in a wood just across the river. In the 17th Century the Old Hall was the residence of the Bannisters from whom it descended to the Croasdales. It is now owned by Mr. John Waddington, who has effected a good work of restoration and converted a ruin into a charming residence.

At Waddow—which in later days was also styled a "Manor" —is an interesting house, probably built as a Tempest dower-house. On the death of the last Tempest of Bracewell and the dissolution of his estates, Waddow came to the Weddalls who died out at the end of the 18th Century. It was then purchased by the Garnetts—together with the Manor of Waddington.

Early in the 13th Century a chapel existed at Waddington, probably erected by the Tempests near the Manor house for the use of their tenants. In 1438 a Composition was made between Sir John Tempest, then Lord, and representative Parishioners of Waddington, Bradford and Grindleton, on the one part and the Abbot and Convent of Cockersand, Rectors of the Church of Mitton, on the other part : by which it was agreed that the garth round the chapel of Waddington should be enclosed as a Cemetery and the chapel kept up as a Parish Church at the expense of the inhabitants of the three townships. They were to attend Mitton Church on Good Friday and to find a Holy Water bearer there ; also to assist in keeping in repair the churchyard wall, bell tower and bells, of Mitton Church. A fit Chaplain was to be provided by the Abbot and Convent and by the Vicar of Mitton, who were to give 2 marks yearly for his stipend ; and he was to live in St. Elyn's house and have certain specified lands assigned for his maintenance.

When Cockersand Abbey was dissolved, the Advowson of Waddington was acquired by the Tempests, who all along had had a good deal to say in the appointments of the Chaplains. In 1597, Richard Tempest sold the Advowson to his cousin John Bannister, who conveyed it in 1616 to his brother Richard from whose heirs it was purchased by the Parkers of Browsholme.

VIII.—Bradford.

Bradford—known as West Bradford, to distinguish it from the City of that name—was never granted out, but was held by the de Lascys in demesne.

In 1258, according to the Inquisition taken on the death of Edmund de Lascy, there were in Bradford six free tenants by charter ; 16 bovates of land ; of which was was held by Jordan Boc at a rent of a bundle of bows ; the other 15 each contained 15 acres and paid five shillings rent. There were 100½ acres of assart at fourpence an acre and there were five cottars—and a mill. In the 16th Century the principal family were the Knolls who lived at Bradford Eaves now called Eaves Hall. The old house was pulled down in the middle of the last century and re-built : this structure has in turn been removed by the present owner, Mr. Burton, who has erected a very fine but somewhat incongruous mansion on the site.

IX.—Grindleton.

Grindleton the pre-Conquest head of the Manor was discarded as such by the de Lascys in favour of Slaidburn. It—like Bradford—was retained in demesne and not granted out. In 1258, at Edmund de Lascy's death, there was a mill there, worth £6 yearly; 24 bovates of land were held in bondage—each containing 12 acres : each bovate paid 16 pence a year and had to make three cartings yearly to Pomfret and ought to plough one day and mow nine days in autumn. There were 99 acres of assart—and no cottars.

The principal family in the 16th Century were the Foules, who represented the township as Judicators or Doomsmen at the Slaidburn Court Baron. Thomas Foule dying in 1535 left three daughters, the youngest of whom married Edward Waddington of Halifax. Their son, Thomas Waddington, added much to the estate which passed 100 years later by marriage to the Holdens of Chaigley, and from them to the family of Brockholes. The ancient deeds (going back to the 13th century) are now in the possession of Mr. Fitz-Herbert Brockholes of Claughton. From a younger branch of this Waddington family descends the present owner of Waddington Hall.

X.—Bashall.

The Charter Roll of 1251 contains a grant to Edmund de Lascy, Earl of Lincoln, of Free Warren in his demesne lands, among which Bashall is named. Two years later, by deed dated at Bashall 1253, Edmund grants and confirms to Thomas Talbot the Manor of Bashall in Fee Farm at a yearly rent of £8.10s.7d. payable at the feast of St. Giles (September 1st). Before this date, Thomas Talbot (who had been Constable of Clitheroe Castle) had acquired land within Bashall ; to this his son, Sir Edmund, added largely by purchase until he had acquired practically all the land within the Manor.

Edmund Talbot received from the King a grant of Free Warren in Bashall by charter dated at Stirling 30th July, 1304—in recognition no doubt of his services against the Scots. In the same year his son and heir, John, was born : and he himself was knighted on the same occasion as Edward, Prince of Wales. Passing over five generations we come to the summer of 1465 when Sir Thomas Talbot proved his Yorkist sympathies by taking a leading part in the capture of King Henry VI. For this act of so-called treachery, Sir Thomas received the curse of King Henry and rewards from King Edward. Among the latter was the remission of the yearly rent of £8.10s.7d. due to the King for Bashall. The curse, according to tradition, foretold nine Talbot Lords of Bashall—wise men and fools alternately—and then extinction. It is not easy to prove the fulfilment of the curse as, after five generations only, the family merged in heirs female : but it may be noted that, during the three centuries that have elapsed since the extinction of the Talbots, the Manor of Bashall has but twice descended from father to son.

On the death of Thomas Talbot in 1619, Bashall passed to his two daughters—Elizabeth, wife of Theobald, Viscount Bourke of Mayo, and Margaret, wife of Colonel William White of Duffield, in Derbyshire, a clerk in the Court of Wards. Margaret had no issue. She bequeathed her moiety to her husband, who bought the other moiety from his brother-in-law, Lord Mayo, and married again. Colonel White was a man of some importance. He joined the Parliamentary Party, acted as Secretary to Sir Thomas Fairfax and sat as Member for Pomfret in the Long Parliament. In 1647 he purchased the Manor and Palace of Bishopthorpe, near York, and added largely to the buildings there. By his will, dated 6th September, 1660, White bequeathed Bashall to his wife for her life, with remainder to his nephew, John Ferrers, and his heirs. John Ferrers died in 1704, and was succeeded by his son, William, who died childless : and Bashall passed to his nephews, Richard Walmesley and Walter Joddrill, who made a partition of the estate. The Hall fell to Walmesley whose arms appear over the entrance to the Great Hall. I have an interesting letter of Walmesley's written in 1745 from Carlisle, when he was acting as a Doctor with the Royal Army. Walmesley died in 1767, leaving an only daughter, Margaret, wife of Hugh Hughes Lloyd of Plymog. She and her husband mortgaged the estate and after their death it was sold in 1806 to James Taylor, Esquire, of Whalley, who also bought the Joddrill moiety.

XI.—Slaidburn.

Out of the Parish of Slaidburn were carved the following Manors :—Rushton, Hamerton, Easington, Battersby, Newton and Knollmere.

Of the township of Slaidburn the greater part remained in demesne, in the Lord's hands. The Inquest of 1258 gives the following survey :—

A Mill, value £4.

30 Acres Arable and 4 acres Meadow in demesne at 4 pence an acre.

3 tenants by charter namely :—

Elias of Knoll holds 30 acres at a rent of 12 barbed arrows.

Walter son of William of Newton holds 40 acres, rent 12 pence.

Geoffrey of Mereley holds 15 acres, rent 5 shillings.

30 bovates of land each containing 6 acres, at 4 pence an acre.

There are men who hold of the assarts freely, not by charter—316 acres.

4 cottars who pay 3s.2d. a year, to the value of 1 acre of land.

Stephen of Hamerton holds all Hamerton by Charter and pays 8 shillings for everything.

The Church of Slaidburn was an ancient foundation. The advowson was granted by Hugh de la Val (1115—1135) to the Priory of St. John of Pomfret. Prior Fulk, between 1231 and 1234 demised it at a yearly rent of 6 marks to Stephen, clerk of Hamerton. After the Dissolution, the Advowson vested in the Crown and was sold to the Marsden family and later to the Wigglesworths who owned the Townhead estate on the outskirts of the village. It is now held by Mr. King-Wilkinson of Whiteholme, a considerable landowner in this Parish.

XII.—Rushton.

The whole of Rushton "except 2 bovates of land which I retain in my hands for the use of my foresters" was granted by Robert de Lascy about 1190 to the Abbey of Kirkstall—together with pasturage in Bolland for 160 mares with their foals up to 2 years and 200 cows with their calves up to 3 years. About ten years later Roger de Lascy, son of Robert, confirmed the gifts of his father and grandfather and gave to Kirkstall the two excepted bovates on condition that the Monks should find two foresters to keep the forest of Bolland. Stephen of Hamerton, at the same time, granted the Monks 20 cart loads of hay out of Hamerton yearly. The Kirkstall Cartulary contains interesting notes as to boundaries and various encroachment on the wastes over which the Monks had rights of pasturage.

At the Dissolution, the Grange of Rushton was bought by Ralph Greenacres and eventually passed into the hands of the Johnsons, a Preston family, who entered their Pedigree in the Lancashire Visitation of 1665. Alexander Johnson, of Rushton Grange, was High Sheriff of Lancashire in 1688, and died 20th August, 1741, aged 90. His son, Alan Johnson, married Elizabeth Lawson, a Wakefield lady, and moved to Wakefield where he died in 1749.

Rushton Grange was sold to the Wigglesworths and by them to the Towneleys some 80 years ago. It is now in course of demolition—a nice old house with many interesting 17th century features—and the whole area is to be submerged to supply Blackpool with water.

Adjoining Rushton Grange is Stocks-in-Bolland, also to be submerged, and the little Church of Dale Head, a parish carved out of Slaidburn 50 years ago.

XXIII.—Hamerton.

Hamerton was from a very early period the seat of an important family. We have seen that in 1258 Stephen of Hamerton held all Hamerton by Charter : but the date of the charter is unknown. The earliest record is a grant to Kirkstall Abbey of 20 cart loads of hay, made at the end of the 12th century by Stephen, son of Hugh of Hamerton. This Stephen is a witness to several late 12th century charters : and his brother Orme of Hamerton, between 1211 and 1220, gave two acres of land in Cheatale, Clitheroe, "to God and S. Nicholas and the house of Edisford and the leprous brethren there for the health of my soul and for the souls of Avice my wife, Stephen my brother, John my son and Amabel my daughter."

Another Stephen of Hamerton was sued at York in 1267 for detaining chattels of William de Tabley. He did not appear to answer the charge and had before made many defaults. The Sheriff, who had been ordered to distrain, passed on the order to the Bailiff of Staincliff. The Bailiff reported that Stephen held nothing in his Bailiwick. But evidence was given that Stephen held two carneates of land and 60 beasts—oxen, cows and horses—by which he could be distrained : so the order to the Sheriff was repeated. When Stephen did eventually appear he won his case.

Those were lawless times. In 1278, John, son of this Stephen of Hamerton, was indicted for murder—he absconded and was outlawed. His elder brother, Richard, also made a bolt but was caught : and at the York Castle Gaol Delivery was brought up for trial. He said that he was a clerk and should not answer in that Court. Whereupon came the Dean of Christianity and Procurator of Lord Walter, Archbishop of York, and claimed him in the name of his Lord as a Clerk. A Jury was called to enquire into the matter, who found him not guilty of the murder but guilty of receiving John, son of Stephen of Hamerton, the murderer. On that charge he was handed over to the Dean. This Richard succeeded to the estates on his father's death : and also to the Rectory of Slaidburn which, as we have seen, was demised to his father in 1234.

The Hamerton pedigree as published is appalling in its inaccuracies : but time does not admit of its discussion here. By a succession of good marriages the family acquired vast estates and it is a tradition that they could ride from Slaidburn to York on their own land.

The end of their greatness came with the Pilgrimage of Grace. Sir Stephen Hamerton joined the rebels—the Commons as they styled themselves—and he and his neighbour Nicholas Tempest of Catlow were hanged, drawn and quartered, at Tyburn—and their estates forfeited. Henry Hamerton, his only son, died of grief on the day of his father's death, leaving two daughters. Part of the estates—Hellifield Peel—was afterwards bought by Sir Stephen's brother, Richard, whose last male heir died 30 years ago, leaving an only daughter.

Hamerton Hall seems to have fallen into ruin and Sir Stephen resided at Wigglesworth, some miles away. Hamerton was sold in 1548 to Oliver Breres, a member of an old Lancashire family, Mayor of Preston in 1558. He built the present Hall at Hamerton, with which is embodied remains of the older house. The Breres family remained here until the latter part of the 17th century, when the then Oliver Breres sold Hamerton to Humphrey Chetham of Manchester and moved with his family to Leeds. The estate now belongs to the Chetham Hospital Trustees.

XIV.—Easington.

The Manor of Easington was in 1284 held by Adam of Wannervill, one of the de Lascy tenants in the Honor of Pomfret. In 1324, when Bolland was in the hands of the Crown owing to the rebellion of Thomas of Lancaster, another Adam paid half a mark for respite of homage at the Bolland Court Baron. But they never resided here. In the 16th century the Manor was held by the Bannisters of Altham. Storth, which formerly belonged to the Knoll family and afterwards to the Parkers, is now owned by Mr. Peel, of Knowlmere : the old Manor house, by Mr. King-Wilkinson.

XV.—Knollmere.

The Manor of Knollmere was part of the holding in Newton of Elias of Knoll, for which in 1258 he paid a rent of 12 barbed arrows. His son Elias held Newton with Battersby in 1284 and in Kirkby's Inquest he is called Elias of Thornley. The Manor of Thornley, near Chipping, was held by the Knolls until the 16th century. Elias the son had several sons and large estates. His eldest son (Rayner), who was Lord of Hellified, died without issue and was succeeded there and in Bolland by his brother, another Elias, who died leaving an only daughter Katherine ; she married Adam of Hamerton and brought Hellified Peel and Knollmere to that family.

On the attainder of Sir Stephen Hamerton his estates were split up. Foulscales in Knollmere, which for several generations had been farmed by the Parkers, was sold to Robert Parker (whose grandfather came from Browsholme) in whose family it remained for many generations. The Manor of Knollmere was granted by the Crown to Cuthbert Musgrave. It is now owned by Mr. Peel, whose great uncle purchased it from the Duke of Buccleugh.

XVI.—Battersby.

The last of these ancient estates or Manors is Battersby—the very name of which has perished.

Battersby was included with Newton in 1284 in the holding of Elias of Knoll. By deed dated 20th August, 1333, Richard of Knoll, Lord of Battersby, granted land there to Richard his son and the heirs of his body. Roger son of this young Richard occurs as Roger of Battersby on the Poll Tax of 1377. His great-great-grandson Richard Battersby in 1497 settled his Manor of Battersby on his nephew—another Richard—and his heirs. The last named Richard died in 1530, his son and heir, Nicholas, being then over 21. The Manor of Battersby was then held of Stephen Hamerton, Esquire, by a rent of a pair of spurs and a barbed arrow.

Nicholas the heir was an outlaw—having got into trouble for murdering a neighbour, Ralph Parker. But in March, 1531, he received the King's Pardon and settled down on his estate.

William Battersby, who died in 1587, held the Manor of the heirs of Simon Knowles, Knight, as of their Manor of Wolf House in free socage by a yearly rent of an arrow called "le Brode Arrow". It is interesting to note that, after the attainder of the Hamertons, the connection of the Knolls of Thornley with Battersby was again put on record. Soon after this, Battersby was sold and the family moved into Cornwall where they recorded their Pedigree at the Visitation of 1620.

The Manor was bought by Tempest Slinger of Catlow in Bolland. He was the son of Henry Slinger of Little Hooton who inherited a moiety of Catlow from his mother, Elizabeth Tempest, sister and co-heir of Nicholas Tempest. Margaret, the other sister, bequeathed her moiety also to Henry Slinger "because he was so like her dear brother". These ladies were the grand-daughters of Nicholas Tempest—called The Sufferer—who, as already stated, was executed at Tyburn for his share in the Pilgrimage of Grace.

Tempest Slinger dropped the name Battersby and the estate has since been called Dunnow, from a steep cliff that overhangs the Hodder. His grandson, another Tempest Slinger, left Dunnow to the Parkers—to the exclusion of his right heirs. These Parkers died out 80 years ago and the estate is now held by Mr. King-Wilkinson.

XVII.—Forest.

Having now discussed the ancient Parishes of Mitton and Slaidburn and the estates held by charter from the de Lascys, there remain some 40,000 acres in Bolland and the contiguous waste of Chippingdale (Little Bolland)—4664 acres—which constitute the Forest or Chace of Bolland.

The Halmote or Chief Court of Bolland is, and usually has been, held at Slaidburn, though occasionally in old days at Waddington. The Woodmote was held at Burholme and later at Whitewell. At Whitewell was the Manor House (now an Inn) and Chapel. The Court Rolls are kept in an oak chest at a public-house—the Hark-to-Bounty—at Slaidburn. There is a good roll for 1390-92 ; and a complete series from 1521 onwards.

There were in the Forest two deer parks or launds ; at Leagram in Little Bolland ; and at Radholme which adjoins Browsholme. The rest of the Forest was divided up into vaccaries and pastures, which were farmed out to various tenants and held by generations of the same family without change. In 1258 there were seven vaccaries, but others were formed in process of time.

The stock was supplied and farmed out by the Lord—that is to say the cattle. The Ministers accounts show some interesting accounts of these cattle, which were supervised in old times by a Storer. In 1422 the stock comprised 9 bulls, 179 cows and heifers, 42 young oxen, 44 bullocks and 150 calves. Of these there was one bull and 42 oxen at Leagram and the rest was distributed among eight vaccaries :—Battris, Burholme, Browsholme, Greystonleigh, Lickhurst, Eshknot, Harden, and Stapleoak. There is no mention of sheep in these lists : this was essentially a cattle-raising district, true to its name.

The Forest was divided, for sporting and other purposes, into four Wards, with one or more Foresters for each ward :—Bashall-ward, Slaidburn-ward, Harrop-ward, and Chipping-ward.

In Chipping-ward was the Park of Leagram. This was farmed out at an early period to the de Hoghtons and later to the Sherburnes who eventually purchased it. It passed with Stonyhurst to the Welds of Lulworth and was settled on a younger son of that family. The present owner, Mr. John Berkeley-Weld is a grandson of the late John Weld of Leagram.

Of the Vaccaries I will only mention Greystonleigh, for centuries farmed by Parkers, part of which was bought early in the 17th century by Henry Farrer—ancestor of our President, Lord Farrer. It now belongs to Lord Derby.

In Harrop-ward was the Vaccary of Harrop and Nettilcarr. Harrop-hall is a quaint old house which was owned in the 17th century by the Moore family—who came from Suffolk. They entered their Pedigree at Dugdale's Visitation of Yorkshire in 1664. After them came the Leighs and then the Wrights.

In Slaidburn-ward there were seven vaccaries. Of these I will only name : (1) Harden which was held by a branch of the Parkers of Browsholme. The last of them to live at Harden was Captain Robert Parker—a great walker : who lost so much money in walking matches—and other pursuits—that he had to sell his estates to the Towneleys. (2) Another vaccary was Stapleoak. This from a very early period was farmed by the Martons. About 1665 William Marton moved to near Lancaster. His son, Oliver, was a Barrister and bought Capernwray, near Lancaster, where his descendants now live. I am aware that the Capernwray Martons have registered a pedigree showing descent from William son of Lionel Marton of Marton in Yorkshire : but Lionel Marton had no son William and if he had had such a son he would have been over 90 when Oliver, first of Capernwray was born.

Last comes Bashall-ward. Here was the Park of Radholme from which, as the Park-keepers, the Parker family derive their name and arms. Richard and John Parker were of Radholme in

This photograph of the **Whitewell Inn** links the old and the modern way of travelling. The Inn has long been a favourite place for refreshment of wayfarers and their horses.

Often wrongly referred to as the Whitewell Swing Bridge, this bridge is really a spring, or suspension, bridge. It was a hundred feet long and some twelve feet above the Hodder, close to the Whitewell Inn. In July 1906, when about fifty trippers were on it, the bridge broke in two places and plunged them into the river, luckily without loss of life.

The **Coach and Horses Hotel**, Main Street, Bolton-by-Bolland, bathed in sunshine in 1933

Bolton-by-Bolland's long-established stocks and cross viewed in the 1920s. The coffee tavern would later become a house.

1393 and had also a lease of the adjoining vaccary of Browsholme, which is described in 1418 as having been recently stocked with cattle. In 1434, Robert Parker was appointed Parker of Radholme by patent : and, though apparently superseded in that office, he continued to farm and reside at Radholme Laund until 1479. To him succeeded Christopher his son, whose male heirs flourished at Radholme till the death of Anthony Parker in 1603. Anthony left two daughters—Ann wife of Edward Scarisbrick of Scarisbrick, and Margaret, wife of John Parker of Bradkirk, who held the Laund until the expiration of the 40 years lease, when it reverted to the Lord.

The Duchy records show that the old lease of Browsholme to Richard and John Parker was renewed from time to time for periods of 20 years until 1507. In that year there was trouble in Bolland. A Commission under Sir Richard Emson had been ordered to re-assess the various rentals and, promising that the deer should be kept in better control, they raised all the rents. The tenants in a body gave notice that they would give up their farms. Upon this fresh Commissioners were appointed who reported as follows :—

"As touching the enprowments and increses made by Sir Richard Emson and other Commissioners by his comandement in Bowlande so it is that we have viewed the lands wherein the said late enprowments were made : and for as moche as it was promysed the tenants and fermors of Bowlande . . . that the dere there shulde by mynyshed and also that they shulde be suffered so to inclose their grounds that the dere might be kept out of them at all times —as by bills by the said late Commissioners made to diverse of the said tenants it doth appere. Which promises be not observed . . . . . for ever sith that time hiderto, Sir Edward Stanley, Knight, Maister of the game ther, wolde not suffer the said tenants to enclose any parcel of the said ground but that the Rede dere and also the falowe dere may have recourse to the said ground at all times without lett : ne wod not suffre any of the said tenants to drive them out : and also that no corne can be sowen there for their relief but the dere destroith it : which caused the said tenants to make exclamation and complaint. Wherfor we . . . viewde the said grounde and what of this enprowment might stand and the dere is continued and therupon made a remembrance as herafter followeth particularly in this book : and as moche we think will stande and the residue will not. And if the dere be clerly put away all the said enprowments will stand good."

Then follows a detail of each vaccary and farm, with statement as to reductions advised. Leagram had been raised from £13.6s.8d. to £20, and Sir Richard Sherburne would give up the farm unless he could have it for £16.13s.4d. "which is thought dere enough."

A new lease of Nether Browsholme (the present house) was thereupon made to Edmund Parker at a slightly increased rent. On his death in 1546 his widow claimed to be admitted tenant by custom of the country, stating that her late husband and his ancestors had been tenants time out of mind and that he had expended large sums on buildings—as the present Hall shows. In 1603, Thomas Parker (grandson of Edmund) purchased the freehold of both Nether and Over Browsholme from the Crown, as well as other lands in the Forest, which have remained vested in his descendants. In 1824 Thomas Lister Parker sold the estates with the house and its contents to his first cousin, Thomas Parker, great uncle of the present owner.

Successive generations of Parkers have held the office of Bowbearer, for which their residence on the spot eminently fitted them. But in no sense, since 1660, has it been hereditary as sometimes alleged.

I will conclude with an extract from a Survey of the Chace of Bolland—part of the possessions of Charles Stewart the late King—made on the 12th day of October, 1652 :—

"The Chace of Bolland was held of the Crown as part of the Duchy of Lancaster by several tenants in Lease, but now for the most part the said lands are held in fee farm being sold to the respective tenants by King James and King Charles as appeareth by divers letters patent. That which now remaineth in lease and in present possession of the State conteyneth as followeth :

[Here follow particulars of 19 tenancies.]

The Officers belonging to the Chace, as we are informed, are a Bowbearer and a Chief Steward.

The Bowbearer hath had heretofore a certain fee out of the rent of the Chace but for divers years last past there hath not been any fee allowed.

By the Chief Steward is yearly kept 2 Swainmote or Woodmote Courts, 2 Courts Leets and 2 Courts Barron, to which the Inhabitants of Bolland are to do sute and service, in which all such as felled any woods, without licence, killed any deer were fined—also all actions under the sum of £2 were tried. The Steward's fee being fourpence for the entering of anie action.

The profits of which Courts, as fines and amercements, we estimate to be now worth communibus annis £1. The other casual profits arising within the said Chace—as waifs, estrays, fellons goods, deodands, fellons de se—are collected by a bayliffe and do amount communibus annis to £3.

The other Officers of the Chace are 12 Keepers, who were appointed for the keeping of the deer both red and fallow. The keeper of the fallow deer was allowed the keeping of two horses yearly . . . also a certain house known by the name of the Whitewell house or lodge, wherewith he hath also part of a house in the tenure of Widow Seed with a barn thereto belonging, a litle piece of ground adjoyning to the westend of Whitewell house and incompassed from the Green by an hedge. Which premises are now in the tenure of William Knipe as Keeper : which we take be worth per annum £2.

. . . . . .

The several tenants, as well fee farmers as lease-holders, within the said Chase are bound by the custom thereof . . . . to suffer the deer to go unmolested into their several grounds and are also stinted in their outgrounds, everyone knowing their stint which he is not to exceed.

They are also fined by the Court if any of them without lycense keep any dog bigger than will go through a stirrup to hunt the deer out of their corne.

The said fee farme lands so stinted for the herbage of the deer we value to be worth per annum £20.

There are of Redd deer of all sorts vizt., stags, hynds and calves, in number 20 which we value to be worth in money £20.

There is also within the chace of all sorts of Fallow deer about the number of 40 which we value to be worth £20."

The last of these deer were destroyed in 1805. Others have been introduced in recent years.

The dog stirrup produced appears to date from the 14th century. It was last used in 1780 when John Parker of Browsholme was elected Member of Parliament for Clitheroe in opposition to the nominee of the Ladies of the Honor. The Ladies, out of spite, ordered that a valuable pack of beagles kept at Browsholme should be tested by this stirrup and, failing to pass the test, the beagles were destroyed.

CHAPTER II.

THE EARLY HISTORY OF BOLLAND BEFORE DOMESDAY BOOK.

Lancashire and the North West of England as a whole share in a general obscurity about events and conditions before the time of the Norman Conquerors. Most of what can be said about the early history can be found in such works as the *Victoria County History*. There we read that what we now call Lancashire was once part of a region never thoroughly colonised by Rome but garrisoned and patrolled by the Roman Legions ; in fact, the Roman road from Ribchester to Lancaster passes through Bolland, wild and deserted as it must have been. That the Romans were not the first to tread this ground we know from the existence of the Bleasdale Circle, a Woodhenge that belongs to the Bronze Age. Then the witness of Celtic names takes us back to pre-Roman times : the river *Hodder*, Bolland's own river and one of the loveliest in England, derives from Celtic words meaning the peaceful or pleasant stream ; and there is a *Mellor* or bare hill near Dunsop Bridge at the beginning of the Trough of Bolland. It is true that Bolland is richest in Scandinavian and Saxon names, but even one British name would be enough to prove British influence in the region.

Are there any definite signs that primitive man lived in Bolland ? The late Colonel Parker claimed to have found a good specimen of an ancient earthwork above Easington Green. Unfortunately, this has been ploughed over during the last war.

There is also a rough stone circle on top of the fells above Easington, like the remains of an ancient fort and watch-tower. To the east of these on Waddington fell there is a most extraordinary assembly of tall bee-hive tumuli, built of rough stones, but so high and well-built that their purpose is hard to explain. Some day these may be explored.

In a later chapter will be found a description of what may well be an ancient British camp site at Castlestead, on the high land at the end of Burnslack Valley, near Chipping. The fact that excavation has proved the existence of a Bronze Age burial at the Bleasdale Circle not far away shows the presence of the Ancient Britons on these hillsides.

It may be useful to record here that there are some unusual long mounds on the top of Birkett. It does not appear likely that these mounds have ever been explored, although we know that in recent years the spade has brought to light not only some of the story of our ancestors but even vast treasures, hidden for centuries. There are various reasons why exploration of the past is sometimes difficult to undertake.

Through the interest of Captain Frank Mitchell there has recently been some digging at the Fairy Holes, a cave above Whitewell.

The Fairy Holes were excavated in 1946 by a team of skilled workers and an account of the work was published by Reginald C. Musson, entitled *A Bronze Age Cave Site in the Little Bolland Area*[1]. A few fragments of pottery enabled the experts to decide that this site had been inhabited during the Bronze Age.

The Roman Road through Bolland.

A book published in 1746 bearing the title *The Roman Antiquities of Overborough* was the work of a Bolland author, the Rev. Richard Rauthmell, and gave the first account of a Roman road running from Ribchester northwards through Bolland. (It may be of interest to note that in his preface Rauthmell gives the spelling *Bolland*, which is the earliest form in print.)

Learned historians have fixed the date of this road as the year 79 A.D. when the Roman general Agricola subdued Wales and the north. The road leaves Ribchester and sets out towards the north. It travels to Jeffrey Hill on Longridge Fell and then forks towards the Hodder, which it crosses below Doeford Bridge. The modern road below Cow Ark follows the old road for quite a distance. On the high ground above Browsholme the road passes Crimpton, Birkett, and then goes to the Hodder again by Knollmere. It then heads for the hills again at Croasdale. It continues up Croasdale, meeting the track to Hornby by the Lancashire and Yorkshire boundary.

Rauthmell says : "This military way enters Yorkshire a little below Dowford bridge, and proceeds on a direct line on the north side of Newton and Slaitburn through Crossa Greet. It is very apparent on the north side of Tatham Chapel." In a later passage he describes how he surveyed 300 yards of excavated road as soon as it enters Yorkshire, that is by Doeford bridge. The land was being ploughed and the road and its foundations were laid bare. There was a foundation of seven yards width made of pebbly gravel in order to drain the soft and morassy soil. The road itself was of stone slabs—"large broad flat stones", as Rauthmell describes them.

Rauthmell says that he found Roman mounds or *Tumuli* with urns buried in them not far from this same Roman way. He points out that it was a Roman custom to bury the dead by the side of a

[1] *Transactions of the Lancs. & Cheshire Antiquarian Soc.*, 1947, p. 161.

road. Unfortunately he does not state where the urns were found. However he gives a good description of the discoveries.

"Near the military way . . . I have discovered some *Roman Tumuli*. In one of these, the stones being removed, I found three urns, two large ones and a little one, which urns, as I imagined, contained the funeral ashes of husband, wife and child. All these three urns contained ashes, and one little urn held ashes and very little bones." p.22.

His description of the *Tumulus* recalls the appearance of the one already mentioned as a fort or watch-tower on the fell-top above Easington. He writes : "This *tumulus* was an exact circle, 10 yards diameter, and one yard deep, of small stones equal with the surface of the ground about it ; and these three urns were deposited under the stones." p.110.

Dr. Whitaker in his *History of Whalley* mentions that when the road was laid bare near Knollmere there were no signs of wheel-marks upon it.

After the Romans.

The Romans more or less abandoned the north after 385, when the General Magnus Maximus withdrew the garrison. Not a single Roman coin later than 385 has been found on the Roman Wall.

Because the Roman garrisons were withdrawn, this does not mean that the countryside was abandoned to the invasion of Irish pirates from the West, or of Pictish barbarians from the North, or of wild Saxon pirates from the East. There is evidence that civilised life went on in the old Roman towns such as Corbridge, Carlisle, Maryport, and Lancaster, to name but a few. No doubt the native tribes were now better able to organise themselves and to train on Roman lines for their own defence. Moreover we learn from the poet Claudian that when the Emperor Honorius succeeded in 395, he had as his chief commander in the West the energetic and capable Vandal Soldier Stilicho, who restored the Roman power in Britain. We do not know how far north of York Stilicho could affirm his power. An imperial document dating from about 428, the *Notitia Imperii*, would suggest that Rome held a line of forts from the Humber to Kirby Thore (*Bravoniacum*) in the Pennines, no doubt holding the line of the old Roman road from York via Catterick to Carlisle. Brougham (*Brocavum*) near Penrith was garrisoned as late as the end of the century, and this lies on the same line of defence against the North, but it would be a thrill to discover why the main line of the Wall from Carlisle to Newcastle was never restored.

It is to this period of declining Roman power that belongs the mission of St. Ninian to Cumberland and to Galloway. This

Briton of Roman civilisation and of Christian education built his church at Candida Casa in Galloway about the year 397. Candida Casa or Whithern (the White House) with its whitewashed stone wall was to be an enduring monument of Rome north of the Solway.

Perhaps the first Christian missionaries travelled to the north-west along the hillsides of Bolland. Certainly the hill-route to the north would be surer in winter than any roads along the low-lying mosses of the flat countryside.

No other traces of ancient habitation.

It has been argued in the past that the Romans must have had some wayside camps in the Bolland region where the soldiers could halt for the night on a journey through this lonely and probably uninhabited moorland. Captain F. Mitchell has tried to find one such camp above Croasdale, acting on statements made by local men about unusual land formations. However, nothing at all definite or even of small interest was found when the land was "explored"

There is of course always a possibility that some such ancient remains will one day be unearthed.

Information from old names.

That Bolland was indeed a forest with a good growth of trees is shown, partly by old names, and partly because towards the reign of Elizabeth I. we know that trees were rapidly being cleared. A name like Birkett surely refers to birch trees and Ashknott to a hill covered with ash trees. Similarly a name like Stapleoak refers to the stump of a huge forest tree. Some great oaks near Leagrim were in the Ackley. Although the word forest can describe any waste or wild place, it is probable that both the Romans and the Anglo-Saxons found Bolland a real forest, well-wooded.

The Anglo-Saxons.

The Anglo-Saxon invasions open a new period of history in all parts of England ; they bring in what have been called the Dark Ages—dark not so much because they were entirely without enlightenment but because so little of that age is known to us ; they bring in too the incorporation of the North West into a new kingdom of Northumbria, although the boundaries fluctuated in both north and south according to the fortunes of war ; sometimes Cumberland would be lost to the Britons of Strathclyde, or sometimes the land between Ribble and Mersey would pass to the kingdom of Mercia.

The seat of government for Northumbria was finally established at Bamburgh towards 635 by Oswald, who brought St.

Aidan and other Irish Christian missionaries from the island of Hy (Iona). The lands to the west of the Pennines must have seemed remote and unprofitable to such a government. Even the ecclesiastical government never established a see nearer than York, to which North Lancashire continued attached until comparatively modern times.

We have no record of how or when the English settlers either came to Bolland or established their sway over the region. The English generally established a small settlement in a valley with a river. Mitton, Newton, and Slaidburn are examples, but their origin is lost in obscurity. Hamerton and Easington are other examples of settlements that never became even a village.

An uncertain clue to the antiquity of Slaidburn may be found in the carved stone of angel, formerly at Slaidburn but now unfortunately lost. The best work on such remains—*Northumbrian Crosses of the Pre-Norman Age* by W. G. Collingwood[1]—gives a drawing of the Slaidburn stone and dates it before the year 1000 A.D. If this expert opinion is correct, there was a Christian community at Slaidburn at least a century before the Norman Conquest.

Strange as it may seem to modern dwellers in Bolland, it is probable that the few farm-dwellers of Bolland in the days of the English settlers would use Chipping as a market. The word Chipping, derived from Old English Chepin, means market. In the days when distances counted less than now in some ways, and rough roads were taken for granted, the dwellers in the Hodder valley could easily find their way to the market at Chipping. We know how the cattle-ranchers of America think nothing of journeying for a long time with their beasts through the open country. Bolland in those days was similar.

William the Conqueror's survey of England, known as Domesday Book, declares briefly what townships had been included in the "manor of Grindleton", formerly held by Earl Tostig, brother of Harold, the last English King before the Normans. Tostig held most of the north, and Domesday Book tells us that "In Gretlinton Earl Tostig was the overlord." To this overlordship were attached the townships of Bradford, Waddington, Bashall, Mitton, Hamerton, Slaidburn, Battersby, Dunnow, Newton, Bogewurth, Easington, Radom, and Sotelie. So from the Domesday survey we are quite sure that these places were inhabited in the days before the Norman Conquest, and no doubt long before the Norman Conquest.

[1] London. 1927.

The Norsemen.

Yet before we come to the conquest of England by the Duke of Normandy, a word must be said about an earlier conquest of the north by the Norsemen. These hardy invaders began to make inroads into the north-west shortly after 900 A.D. They had already established themselves in northern Ireland and they slowly penetrated the rough or mountainous lands of the north-west. To quote an interesting statement by one historian : "As sheep-farmers, the men who could thrive in Iceland could thrive on the fells and moors of the north, where the Angles had found no land suitable for their corn and cattle."[1]

All students of north-country history know that the Viking invaders have left definite traces of their occupation in the names of many places. There are perhaps less of these names in Bolland than in parts of Lancashire, Cumberland, and other places. Yet the Viking influence is unmistakable.

Take, for example, Bolland names like Oxengill, Hasgill and Brungillmoor. The word *gil* is an old Norse word meaning a narrow valley, and it is to be found attached to streams all over the north-west, more than elsewhere.

Another Norse word that is found wherever Viking settled is *erg*—a hill farm or shieling. Battrix was once Batherarges (explained as *Bothvar's erg* or farm). Cow Ark may be explained in the same way—a hill shelter for cows.

Battersby, the old name for Dunnow near Slaidburn, is probably derived from the words *Bothvar's by*, meaning the homestead of Bothvar, probably a kinsman of the Bothvar at Battrix not far away.

The Norse influence, although real, was not so deep-rooted as to be able to outdo the English. The greater number of Bolland place-names are to be explained by their English origins.

The name Bolland.

In his introduction to Bolland history, Colonel Parker says that Bolland means the land of cattle ; derived from the Norse—*Bu*, meaning cattle. Perhaps Bull-land might be possible, with a similar meaning but English in origin. Bolland was always a stock-rearing country.

[1] From W. G. Collingwood, as above, p. 123.

CHAPTER III.

THE MONKS OF KIRKSTALL ON THE UPPER HODDER.

The Cistercian farmers penetrated into so many of the lonely and wild retreats of the North, that it is not surprising to find trace of them in the remotest and most isolated part of the Hodder valley, as the river first flows down from the hills by Crossagreet. Not much more than a century after the Normans had first invaded and over-run the land, we find Robert de Lacy (1166-1194) making a grant to the monks of Kirkstall of "all Ristune in Bochlande, together with pasture for eight score mares and their foals up to two years and two hundred cows with their offspring up to three years . . . . I reserved, however, two bovates of land at Rishtun which I retain as long as I will for the work of my foresters."[1] This Robert de Lacy, last of the original line, was buried at Kirkstall.

Several documents relating to the tenure of the Kirkstall monks in the Hodder valley have been preserved and published in the Latin text. They are of value to the historian of Bolland, and of great interest to the student of old names. For instance, Gradel, formerly the moor between Crosdale and Hareclough, but now practically forgotten in the district, is found in a Kirkstall document probably about the year 1200. It is the confirmation by Roger de Lacy, who founded a second line of the family, of the grant made by Robert de Lacy, his great-uncle, with the addition of a further privilege, namely that of making cattle folds. " . . . . When they have need of rounding up the young stock, male and female, they may make their folds in Gradale and Crossedale under the inspection of my foresters."[2] The same Roger also surrendered to Kirkstall the two bovates of land kept back by the first grant, on condition that the monks should provide him with two foresters.[3]

John de Lacy, son of the above Roger, succeeded in 1211 and continued his family's tradition of making grants to Kirkstall. The first of these contains an unusually large number of quaint and unfamiliar names, so much so that it was only after a long search and after following many false tracks that a clue was found to the places referred to. The text is as follows : " . . . . all my land which is called Gamellesarges in Bochland, bounded as follows : from the dike of the monks aforesaid up to Wippecloh, and so to

[1] Kirkstall, cclxxxi.

[2] Kirkstall, lxix.

[3] Kirkstall, cclxxxii.

Fulelache, and from the upper part of Fulelache by the upper part of Gamellesarges to Querenstaingile, then coming down by Querenstaingile up to the middle of Essart Andree (Andrew's Stubbings) and from the middle of this Essart straight to the dike of the monks at Elkegile ; and besides this, one acre in the field which is called Maurethuait."[1]

It is likely that all these boundaries, like Rishton Grange, the chief territory of Kirkstall, now lie under the waters of the Hodder dam. Gamellesarges is one of the old farm names of a thousand years ago left by the Norsemen, as are also Querenstaingile and Maurethuaite—the 'arg' or 'erg' (hill pasture), the gill (brook) and the 'thwaite' (clearing) are all unmistakable Old Norse words.

The first clue to deciphering the old landmarks was "the dike of the monks", which was presumed to lie either at the bounds of their lands at Rishton Grange or by their pastures of Gradel and Crosdale. The former was preferred, as being a more likely place for a ditch or a dike than the wide spaces of the moors. This idea was confirmed by the mention of Essart Andree or Andrew's Stubbings, as this name indicated that here the land was being "grubbed and stubbed" or generally cleared for cultivation. Incidentally the use of the word Essart for the clearing of newly enclosed land has its own interest to the student, as it clearly shows the French culture of these Anglo-Norman lords and monks, who drew up the early deeds. In the French language, Essart is now quite obsolete, except in some names of places, although it is commonly found in old writings from the twelfth to the sixteenth century.

Another possible clue is Elkgile, which may be represented on the modern large-scale map by Eak Hill, which rises to the north-west of Rishton Grange. Thirdly, not far from Eak Hill, though on the other side of the river, was Gamble Hole wood, a name which recalls the Gamellesarges of the old text. Another indication of the locality may be had from the mention of Wippecloh, which is probably the same as Whippe Clowe, found in a 1575 boundary, and lying somewhere between Hare Clough and the Hollins.

From these various indications, it seems very likely that the Gamellesarge land, granted to the monks, lay on the rising ground to the west of Rishton Grange. However, as so much of this area now lies submerged, there is only curiosity to promote further research about these old place-names and boundaries.

A further grant from John de Lacy has been largely quoted in its original Latin by the later editors of Whitaker's *Whalley*.

[1] Kirkstall, cccxxxvii.

It gives to the monks all the higher lands to the east of the Hodder in its upper reaches towards Keasden and Bolland Knotts, and including the old hamlet of Stocks in Bolland, now under the water. The deed grants to Kirkstall "all the land with wood and pasture without reservation, which I have held on the eastern part of the water of Hoder in Bowelande, as the said water of Hoder comes down from the higher head of Gradalehals through the grange of the aforementioned monks to the vill of Riston ; and from the aforementioned head of Gradalehals to the higher part of Keseden, by the bounds and divisions between my fee and the fee of William de Mubray ; and from the upper head of Kesedene to the upper head of Rowenumcnothes ; and from the upper head of Rowenumcnothes to the eastern head of Rowenumcnothes, and from the eastern head of Rowenumcnothes to the upper head of Hesebrithehawbroc by the bounds and divisions between my fee and the fee of William de Percy ; then from the upper head of Hesebrithehawbroc, as the water of Hesebrithehawbroc goes down into Thirnesetgilebroc ; and from Thirnesetgilebroc as the water of Thirnesetgilebroc goes down into the water of Hoder by the vill of Riston."[1]

No cattle were to feed within these bounds except those of the monks, and if any entered they could be put in a pinfold until redeemed. The only right retained by the overlord was that of hunting wild beasts.

The old name of Rowenumcnothes has survived as Bowland Knotts in one place and as Knotteranum in another. The stream called Hesebrithhawebroc (Hesebert's Hill Brook) has survived to modern times through the Hesbert Hall farm by the side of it and by the Hesbert Hall Syke. It is a pity that throughout Bolland the old Hawes or Hills were first spoiled as names by the useless addition of Hill, so that instead of saying the Hawe, people began to say Hawe Hill, and a later and more ignorant generation made the name into Hall Hill.

The Thirnesetegile of the old charter was in later times known as Bridge House Beck and flowed into the Hodder below Stocks in Bolland. Already in the thirteenth century the meaning of the word 'gill' must have been obscure to some people as the English word 'brook' was added to describe it.

It may be noted that the modern boundary of Gisburn Forest passes along the beck or the brook by Hesbert Hawe.

[1] Kirkstall, cclxxxviii.

TWO KIRKSTALL DOCUMENTS ON THE FOREST LANDS.

Among the Kirkstall deeds are two valuable documents which relate to a survey of different lands in various parts of the Hodder valley, ranging from Crosdale to Burholme. They contain useful lists both of places and of persons.

"The investigation relates that the Lords of Bouland have made the following enclosures during the last twenty years in various places :

at Grysehurst, according to estimate 40 acres
pasture of Batharar 24 acres.
(Today these estates are part of Battrix above Dunsop Bridge)
at Stapelak 24 acres ; meadow of Stapelak 5 acres
at Byrolm 6 acres
Stotclos 30 acres. (This estate is across the river from Burholme).
Horsclos de Byrolm 10 acres
Stakker de Byrolm 12 acres
Field of William de Lond 5 acres
Son of Robert del Clogh 1 acre
John Lax i acre
Robert Chapon 1 acre
Henry Brand ½ acre
Romuelstede ½ acre
Adam de Raingyll, sunfeld 6 acres
the same elsewhere in the same holding 2 acres

Horse closes of the Abbot of Kirkstall in Bouland :
one at Bathersby in Brungalmore, Newton
another at Wodhows near Slayborn
a third in Gradhall near Flakclogh
and in Crosdale one fold for animals and one lodge for the shepherds and growing plants, by name Harclogh in Crosdale, and William del Loghe keeper, namely in the 40th year of King Edward III (1366).

And it should be noted that in all the said lands we should have right of common pasture for a certain number of different animals of our own."[1]

The following document contains some of the same names of places and of persons as the one translated above, but it has also some additional information :

"Memorandum of land newly enclosed in Bouland.
In the Stotclos 24 acres, namely between Byrolm and Redsyk.
In Bryolm 20 acres of vaccary (cow-pasture)

[1] Kirkstall, ccccxxix.

In Langdenholm 4 acres near Stotclos
In a certain close near Harden 20 acres
In the Redsykgraynes 40 acres
(This would be on the land above the modern Hodder Bank).
In Brokholehyrst 30 acres
In Greyshyrst 30 acres, namely in Batharars.
In the Brungylmore 2½ acres, namely in Newton
In the meadow of Batharars 24 acres
In Stapelake 24 acres
Field of William de Lound 5 acres, namely in Slaytborn
Son of Robert del Clogh 1 acre
John Lax 1 acre
Robert Chapon 1 acre
Henry Brand ½ acre
Routhemelstede ½ acre
Adam de Rayngyll in his field 6 acres
The same elsewhere on the same holding 2 acres
All the above in Slaytborn
At Fynas 6 acres
In the fold of the Abbot of Kirkstall at Wodhous 1 rood
In all 355 acres
Also in the park of Basscholf at the time of Lord Henry de Lascy 200 acres and a half.
Also of Gradalhous, which was once called Randolfbothe, according to estimate 40 acres."[1]

These two surveys made by the monks of Kirkstall show that their interest in the Hodder valley extended as far as Burholme, and even into the Langden valley at Stapleoak. As the law then stood, those who made appropriations or enclosures on commons or forest were obliged to leave sufficient common for general use and to allow free access.

Of the ancient names here mentioned several are of interest. Stapleoak or Stumpoak must originally have been marked by a tree root of unusual size, probably a relic of the ancient forest like the great black stumps that were frequently dug up in Chipping Moss, according to Weld's *History of Leagram*. This stump must have been a real landmark for it was marked by other references to the place as the 'Root'; hence Dunsop Bridge Chapel was often called Root Chapel and a farm nearby as Root Farm. Where was this great oak root?

Fynas is the old way of writing Phynis. Its origin is obscure, although it may derive from the Old English *fina*, a Woodpecker. Green woodpeckers are found in Bolland.

[1] Kirkstall, ccccxxxi.

Gradalhous, mentioned as being formerly known as Randolfbooth. is not easy to identify. Randolfbooth or Randolf's farm represent a type of name not common in this part of the country. It is possible that Gradalhous is the old name for Croasdale House.

These later Kirkstall documents (probably 1367) give evidence about Grisehurst and Battrix (Batherars) similar to that of Abbot Lyndsay of Whalley in 1342, except that the Whalley version of Battrix seems older in form. The Abbot wrote that the inhabitants of these places paid tithes to Whalley church, namely "Brenand, Trogh, where those of Whytlidale now dwell, Sikes, Harden, Stapelhaw, Thorniholme, Grishurste, and Bathirarghes, as the Frythebroke descends into the water of Hodder."[1]

Both Grisehurst and Battrix are names with Norse elements that take us back a thousand years. *Gris* is the Norse word for pig, sometimes used as a person's name. Bathirarghes is taken to be Bothvar's *erg* or hill-farm.[2]

There is no stream called the Frithbrook today. The word *frith*, a wood, and the word *hurst*, a wooded hill, suggest that the locality was richer in trees than it is today.

Captured in the early years of the century by Mr. Buck, a very active Clitheroe photographer, Hammerton (or Hamerton) Hall and the Hammerton family have played a major role in Bolland's story.

[1] Whitaker, i, 328-329. Latin text.

[2] Ekwall.

CHAPTER IV.

ANCIENT BOUNDARIES.

One of the most fascinating tasks for the student of Forest history is the rediscovery of old boundaries and landmarks, which are so clearly set out on many ancient deeds and records, and yet today many of them seem to be forgotten in the countryside. Many of the old names, too, have a peculiar interest of their own—various forms of them appear in different centuries, or sometimes a most curious and unusual name will appear such as Ughtersike above Tarnbrook, a name known only to two or three shepherds, but which can be traced back to the Middle Ages. Some of these old boundary names are so quaintly fashioned and so different from our modern speech that they seem to belong to a completely different language, as Knowenumcnothes by Bolland Knotts, or Sinkan de Beck above Cross of Greet, and indeed many more.

Domesday Book does not mark any boundaries in its description of the Bolland territory. It merely indicates the amount of territory in various districts :

In Gretlintone Lord Tosti has 4 carucates of land. In Bradeforde 2, Widiton 2, Baschelf 4, Mitune 4, Hameretone 2, Slateborne 4, Badresbi 2, Neutone 4, Bogeuurde 2, Esintune 3, Radun 2, Sotelie 3, these lands lie together in Gretlintone.

Badresbi or Battersby was the district round Dunnow near Slaidburn. From its position in the list, the forgotten name of Bogeuurde may be the old Norse farming settlement of Bothvar's Erg, now know at Battrix near Dunsop. It is possible that the name Sotelie is represented today by a group of lands called the Lees, especially as it is named after Radholme.

When we find that the old names are scarcely recognisable to the modern reader, we feel that we are forging a link with the past when we try to make these ancient signs once more have a meaning. The following list of names from the possessions of Henry, Duke of Lancaster, on his death in 1361, contains a number that are not easy to place[1]:

Slayteborne in Bouland with the Forest
Bremund pasture (Brennand)
Roudon (Raddom)
Up. Aldington (Spaldington?)
Maukholes (Mould Holes near Boasden?)
Crombewell (This and the next are one word and near
Holme Browsholme)

[1] Inq. P. Mortem. quoted Gregson, p. 113.

Baxsterhay (Battrix?)
Browesholme
Berkholme (Burholme?)
Eghes (Leghes?)
Latheringrime (Leagrim)
Bernardseles (In Leagrim)
Nicolshey (In Leagrim)
Wardslegh
Hogeking Height (In Leagrim)
Crepingwarde (Chepingward?)
Benteley Close
Graistanley
Peinleighes (Pimlines, Leagrim)
Coswayne
Chipping Crosdale
Neuton
Hamerton
Witton (Waddington?)
Grimlington
Salley mill
Bradeford in Bouland
Bakshelf in Mitton
Withikill (Withgill)

The northern limits of the Forest in the period before 1300 are indicated in the grant of land made by John de Lascy about 1232-1240 to the monks of Kirkstall. In his deed of grant mention is made of the bounds of Kesedene between his fee and the fee of William de Mowbray; and on the north-east of Rowenumcnothes and Hesberthawebrook, the Forest met the bounds of the fee of William de Percy. (See Kirkstall chapter).

One of the most detailed boundary records is printed in Whitaker as a perambulation of the Forest dated Whalley 1483. In fact it only covers part of the Forest bounds, as it is a description of the Castle parish of Clitheroe, or what today is called Whitewell parish. It contains many names which have proved hard to identify, although most of them have been traced after much research.

The account begins at Rawcross, somewhere on Waddington Fell by New-a-Nook, not far from the Moorcock inn. The New Hey Head in the deed was on the hill above New Hey, often mentioned in the old registers of Waddington, but now quite unknown in the district. By detective work on maps and by other lines of enquiry New Hey above Waddington can be certainly identified with the modern Coulthursts. New Hey was a group of homes and not just a single farm.

Description of the Castle Parish Bounds before 1500.

Beginning at Rawcrosse and Newhayhead bounding upon the parish of Slaydburn and from Newhayhead following westward to the Longshaw, and from Longshaw to Cromptendenhead (*Crimpton on the modern map*) and from Cromptendenhead following up the Oakenclough to the height of Kytcholme, and from the height of Kytcholme to Fieldyngcloughhead (*above Burholme*), and from Fieldyngcloughhead to the Deepe Clough head, and from the Deepe Clough head to the water of Hother. (*Deepe Clough is now Robin Clough*).

Then following up the water of Hother to the departing betwixt the Duke's ground called Thorneholme and Hamerton's land, and so unto water of Hother.

(The Hamertons possessed as part of the Knowlmere estate the farm of Netherthorneholme, now called Lower Thorneyholme. Thorneyholme, then part of the Duke of Lancaster's estate, is still separate from the Lower Thorneyholme.)

And so following the water of Hother into Langden water, and from thence following the meres (*bounds*) between Borholme and the Stod Close unto the Reed Syke, following up the Reed Syke to the height of Todrigge.

(It may be noted here that it is not easy to say where the Stod Close or Stud Fold was exactly situated. The Kirkstall monks wrote that Stot Close was between Byrolm and Redsyk and that Langdenholm was near Stotclose. Thus it would seem that the Farm Hodder Bank is very likely on the site of Stotclose.)

So following Todridge as heaven water deales unto the head of Brandslack (*Burnslack*) brook to the parish of Chipping, and so from thence to the head of the Threapleigh, and from Threapleigh unto Peacock Clough, so following Peacock Clough into Chipping Brook, and so following Chipping Brook to the Park Yate at Laygrim at Chipping Brook.

(Most of these names are familiar in the Leagrim and Chipping district today, although from the above description Peacock Clough is now Dobsons Brook. The Leagrim Park Gate probably stood near the present bridge over Chipping Brook.)

And so following from the Park Yate the brook to the head of Hudefield, and so following from the head of Hudefield to the Pale ; and so following from the Pale to the lands of Startevants, so following the lands of Startevants to Chipping Brook unto the foot of the water of Lowde.

(The movement of the boundary line is very peculiar in this part, and the description is complicated, if Pale is interpreted as Pale Farm. Pale no doubt means here just the line of the deer-fence. Even so, it is hard to see why the boundary suddenly leaves the line of the fence, follows Startivant farm fence, joins Chipping Brook again, and then follows the Loud. Probably some extremely old land tenure in Chipping pushed the Forest boundary away from Chipping Brook to the present line of the "Pale".)

So unto the water of Hother, bounding upon the parish of Mitton, and following the water of Hother unto Wierburne foot, so following Wierburne foot to the head of Bashall Park.

(The name Weirburne has been lost. In modern times this stream is called Mill Brook from an old paper mill now vanished.)

And so following the lordship of Bashall and the Duke's land (Browsholme) unto Newhahouse, and from Newhahouse following the devise of the lordship of Bashall and the Duke's land unto the head of Braddop, and from Braddop head to the water side of New Ditch to the head of Newhay.

(The head of Braddup is now marked on the map as Braddup Moss. The difficulty about the boundary here is that it speaks of the separations between the Duchy lands and Bashall Manor. It is probable that these boundaries changed in the period when the Talbots of Bashall were extending their power. However, the head of New Hay must be near Cob Castle.)

So following from the head of Newhay ensuing the Woodward Score to the north end of Whitstonecliffe, as heaven water deals.

(In another chapter there is mention of the Woodwards or Keepers of the Forest, who kept the King's deer on these fells. The name Woodward Score probably means Division of the Forest Keepers—see scear in Old English, meaning a division of land. A similar use of the word Score is seen in the old documents about Crosdale Score—see chapter on Crosdale.)

So following the Woodward Score from the head of Whitstonecliff to Wolfstanbanke as heaven water deals ; so following from Wolfstonebank to the Stone with the Steps, as heaven water deals ; so following from the Stone with the Steps to the height of Swarthow, as heaven water deals.

(Practically all the names mentioned above are now lost, although the line of the boundary can be verified by the survival at Harrop Hall of a field-name, Swarthow meadow, which is on the hill, no doubt called Swarthow or Black Hill before 1500.)

So following from the height of Swarthow to the well in the north end of Swarthow ; so following the well stream from the north end of Swarthow to the Champion Dike bounding upon the parish of Slaidburn aforesaid.

(Long and fruitless inquiry in the district has proved that the name and the memory of a landmark called Champion Dike have quite vanished. This can be readily explained by the fact that since the Middle Ages more and more of Champion has been enclosed, until only a small part at the summit remains today as common. A similar Dike called Harrop Dike is part of the old boundary on the other side of Harrop Fell Brook at Lane Ends. It seems probable that the old dikes on Champion and Harrop today follow the line of the wonderfully straight road from Harrop Hall to Smallden Lane. Curiously enough some farmers in the district have called these long straight dikes "Roman Dikes". Both Champion and Harrop Dikes drain into Fell Brook at Lane Ends.)

So following the Champion Dike to Fellbrig Water ; so following Fellbrig Water up Harrop Dike to the height of Heskin Hill as heaven water deals.

(The old estate of Harrop and Netlycarr—now Harrop Hall and the Cross—was all on the lower side of the present road and Champion common on the other. The traveller along this road and Smallden Lane can still find traces of a wide and long ditch. Heskin Hill is now called Beacon Hill, but the farm nearby called Asker Hill or Adder Hill shows some trace of the old name.)

So following from the height of Heskin Hill to Brynhill Pike, as heaven water deals ; so following from Brynhill Pike to Whitstonecliff, and so from Whitstonecliff to Raw Cross aforesaid.

(From Beacon Hill or Heskin the boundary swings rapidly uphill to the summits of Waddington Fells. The Brynhill of the old boundary is no doubt the 1300 foot summit above what is called today Brown Hill, probably a mistake for the Celtic word Bryn—a mound or hill. A Celtic name is all the more indicated because not far below on the Easington side at Skelshaw are the remains of an ancient British Camp.)

CHAPTER V.

EARLY FOREST RECORDS.

[Translation of Important Bolland Documents—from Whitaker's *Whalley*, vol. i, p. 343.]

[Note.—The Editors of Whitaker published a valuable assortment of records, copied from the originals, and printed for the most part without translation, notes, or commentary. The student must be grateful for this, but in view of the fact that many readers cannot readily interpret the medieval French or Latin of these documents, it was felt by the present authors that a real service would be afforded to many of those interested in Bolland history by providing a translation of these interesting documents. We have omitted some of the technical details because these are available to the trained scholar in the original publication. Some words like *farm* for rent are left as they stand.]

Warrant from John of Ghent, Duke of Lancaster, 1374.

Johan, etc., to our well beloved Milord Wauter Ursewyke our chief Forester of Bouland, greeting. We will and command that thou take from our venison in our chace of Bouland as much as seem good to you for our advantage, and send it to the folk of the country around wherever it may seem best for our advantage and the protection of our venison in those places . . . . Given at our Chastel of Knaresburghe the xv day of September. (The heading in Whitaker suggests that the Forester should send presents of game, but that does not seem the intention.)

Warrant to the Storer (chief cattle-keeper) of Bolland to sell nine colts. Johan, by the grace of God, King of Castile and Leon, Duke of Lancaster. To our dear and well loved William atte Lee our Storour in Bouland greeting. We command you that by the judgment and superintendance of our well beloved Cleric Sir William de Horneby you have sold nine colts from our stud in your keeping, at whatever time and place seem good for our honour and profit, and the same money have delivered to the said Sir William, our Receiver there, in due number. And these our letters will be your warrant. Given, etc. at our Chastel of Pountfreit the xxvii day of July the fifth year of our very revered Lord the King Richard second after the Conquest.

For Thomas Talbot, esquer. Johan, etc. To our well beloved Bachelor Milord Wautier Ursewyk Chief Gardien of our Chace of Bouland greeting. We command you that to our well loved Thomas Talbote you have delivered six oaks suitable for building, which we have ganted him from our gift to be taken in your aforementioned territory . . . Given at Leicestre the first day of August (1382).

Accounts of Henry de Worsley, Storer of Bolland (1422-23).

SCLATBOURNEWARDE.

- 40s. from the pasture of Crossedale granted to Richard Hoghton, son of Henry Hoghton, knight . . . formerly only paying 13s4d.

- 53s4d from the farm of Brennand vaccary granted to Henry Hoghton knight for the term of his life by letters patent at Pontefract on July 1st, 2nd year of Henry V (1414).

- 100s. from the farm of the vaccary of Hieghoke and Randolfboth, granted this year thus and not more, because the Abbot of Kyrkstall has a right of common pasture in them.

- 66s8d from Whytledale vaccary granted to Hy. Hoghton by above letters patent

- 106s8d from Trogh and Sykes vaccary granted to Thomas Bonde for life by letters patent at Westminster March 22nd, second year of Henry V (1422).

- 53s4d from the farm of Stotleclose granted to Henry Hoghton by above letters patent.

- 20s from farm of half Harden vaccary ; the other half for stock cattle.

- nothing from Baterax and Stapilloke vaccaries because they are for stock cattle. Total 22£

HARROPWARD.

- 50s from farm of Harrope and Netylcarre vaccaries granted to Hy. Hoghton as above.

- 26s8d from the farm of pasture of Harrope granted to Henry as above

- 3s from tenants of Chattebourne for common pasture in Sclatebourne with their stock in summer as they have been accustomed from ancient time.

- 2s from the tenants of Sclatebourne for Overshote which the tenants of Holden have had on the pasture of the said tenants of Sclatebourne thus granted them by the Seneschal, hence an increase of 6d. Total 4£ 20d.

BAXSHOLFWARDE.

- 30s from Newehey granted to aforesaid Henry as above.

- 10s from farm of Thorneholme granted to Henry Whytedale this year.

- 18s from the farm of Spersmore granted to Nicholas de Swynehurst for this year.

- 8s8d from the farm of a certain place called Spaldyngtonmonclose granted to the same Nicholas.

- 10s from herbage of a 4th part of Broghseholme of which the other 3/4 are for stock.

- 4£ from the farm of a pasture calle the Leghes granted this year with two places outside Baxsholfswarde and 8 acres of waste which Henry Langtaa recently held enclosed, formerly at 66s8d, And of a certain place called Crumbilholme which John de Threfalle recently held, formerly at 6s8d, thus at the same time granted to the aforesaid Henry as above.

- 33s4d from the farm of Swynhulhurst so granted this year.

- 8£ from the herbage of Radom park so granted to the aforesaid Henry.

- from 3 parts of Broghseholme nothing because they are for stock. Total 17£ 10s.

CHEPYNWARDE.

- 26s8d from the farm of Wardesclogh with 2 parts of Hogekynhey so granted to the aforementioned Henry as above.

- From Nicolhey, the 4th part of Hogekynhey, Bernardclose, Chepynbroke, Grenelaunde, Lathegryme, and Colston, nothing because they are enclosed within the park of Lathegryme.

- 12s from the farm of Wyndhulles thus granted to him reckoning to the end of ten years this being the sixth year by agreement of Richard Hoghton Knight and Thomas Urswyk as appears by an extract of Roger Flore Chief Seneschal shown upon the account of the sixth year of King Henry V.

- 35s4d from the agistment of Fence this year in winter time thus granted to the aforementioned Henry as above, over 32 cows of the King from Birholme, 16 cows of the King from Harden, and 16 cows of the King from Eshenoke (Dinkling Green).

- 6s8d from the winter agistment of the said Fence granted by Henry of Whytledale to different men from the feast of St. Martin within the time of the account to the feast of the Finding of Holy Cross (i.e. November 11 to May 3) next following for having 11 cattle in the said Fence for the same time, an animal at 2d.

- From the farm of one house and garden within Laythegrime park, nothing because it is falling down and is empty.

- 13£ 6s 8d from the agistment of Leagram park granted to Robert Urswyke knight this being the 6th year to be paid at Easter and Michaelmas equally by agreement with Laurence of Hamerton, Thomas of Urswyke, Richard of Knolles, and Michael Levers . . . above 36 oxen of the said Lord the King in winter at 8d and in summer during the agistment at 9d 38 bullocks in winter at 8d and in summer at 18d.

- 5s from the farm of Accornhirst near the park of Laythegryme and recently included in it granted this year to Rd. Henryson.

- 20s from the farm of Brendslake granted to John Parker son of Elias Parker for the term of 20 years . . . this the 4th year, and before it used to return only 16s, thus increase of 4s.

- 5s from the farm of a piece of pasture called Accornhirst close to the said park granted to the same Rd. Henryson and he encloses it at his expense.

- 6s 8d from the herbage of Fence in winter, nothing this year because it is occupied by the King's stock.

Total 18£ 16s 4d

Sale of Stock .... Total 22£ 18s 4d

Stock raising from 5 full ½ and ⅛ vaccaries ... 15£ 3s

- 2s from the increase of the farm of half Lekehirste vaccary granted to John Parker son of Elias Parker (as above).

- 19s 4d from an increase made by the said Chief Seneschall on different vaccaries—John Parker and Richard Parker for the farm of Brogisholm vaccary 3s 4d, granted for 20 years ; William Swynehulhurst for the said vaccary of Fayrakhous and Greystonlegh 3s 4d granted for the same term ; John Greydale for the other half of Greystonlegh 4s, for the same term ; Nicholas Swynhulhurst for half the vaccary of Essheknottes and Denglegrene 3s 4d for the same term ; John Swynhulhurst for Birgholme 5s 4d for the same term . . . . this the 4th year.

Total 16£ 4s 4d

Total Sum received 101£ 11s 8d

Grant of Farm - From the above deduct 20s from the grant of a farm above mentioned under Harropwarde with the figure of 26s 8d from the farm of herbage at Harrop recently granted to various tenants in Gryngleton by the Chief Seneschal, which herbage the Wodewards (Woodwards) held there for 6s 8d a year as a token for their service in guarding the wild beasts of our Lord the King in that place, etc., because the said Wodeward (Woodwards) have had the herbage as they have held it before, namely for 6s 8d . . . . . for otherwise he (they?) would not look after the wild animals . . . . (The Latin is very poor and very involved but seems to justify the retention by the Woodwards of their traditional pasture.)

* * * *

Colonel Parker's account of the Forest farms gives some of the remaining details about Bolland in 1322, namely a list of the cattle, bulls, etc. He draws attention to the fact that sheep are not mentioned.

Two names given above under Baxholfe warde are worth attention because they convey information not found elsewhere : Crumbilholme and Swynhulhurst. Both are names of farms in the

Browsholme area and both places gave their name to families which lived for generations in Bolland before migrating elsewhere. An offshoot of the Crombleholmes is in New Zealand.

Another name worth noting in its old form is Fayrakhous, although this spelling does not make its true meaning any clearer. Two hundred years later it is written Faredelholme or Fayredockhouse, and in modern times as Fair Oak, although the Bolland folk call it Farrick. The explanation that appeals most to the present writers is ***Far-Rake*** or far stream. 'Far from where?' some-one might ask. Probably far from New Laund, from which it was originally farmed no doubt.

Denglegrene for Dinkling-green or the green in the hollow is a very appropriate name, as any visitor to the place can verify. Maybe the original name was Dingle Ing.

The last part of the document, which mentions the Woodwards or keepers from Grindleton throws light on the problem of boundary names as well as on the question of where the deer were kept. From this account it seems likely that Harrop fells were not enclosed at all at this period (1422), and that the tenants of Grindleton had pasture rights there for a small fee. The Chatburn and the Holden farmers, mentioned earlier, would graze upon Champion, although this hill-pasture is not mentioned by name. The Woodwards of Grindleton help to understand a reference in the 15th century boundaries of Whitewell parish (See the chapter on boundaries) where the Woodward Score is mentioned on Waddington fell. The Woodward Score obviously marked one of the limits watched by these Forest keepers.

Under Chippingward the references to Leagrim show that the area of the deer-park land must have been extended only a few years before, because the park is given as a reason why no rent accrues from certain farms. Grenelaunde (mentioned among these farms) was probably the original small enclosure for the deer. The farm now called Chipping Lawnd probably marks this original site of the deer-park of Leagrim.

From other accounts of this period, it is known that besides Leagrim Park there were in Bolland two other principal enclosures for the deer, namely Radholme Park and the New Launde. The first date of appointment for the Keepers or Parkers of Radholme, as given in Whitaker, is 1413 for Robert Mitton, while Richard de Hoghton was appointed to Leagrim in 1410.

It should be noted that close to the New Launde the officers of the Forest had been making extensive repairs and alterations to the Manor and Chapel of Whitewell in the year 1422. New *thak* or thatch was being placed on the chapel and other buildings, and slatestones from Marsden near Colne were being put over the kitchen. The importance of this kitchen may be gathered from the fact that 66 'loads' of slate were carried for it, admitting of course that the amount of a load is not stated.[1]

The exact date of the establishment of this Manor-house and Chapel at Whitewell is uncertain. It became an important centre for the Forest, as the Woodmote Court was held here. Previously the Woodmote or Forest Court had been held at Burholme, as Colonel Parker has pointed out. No doubt there was a Chapel transferred at the same time from Burholme to Whitewell (see chapter on Bolland Chapels). There seems some likelihood that the establishment of the great parks at Radholme and Leagrim, as also of the Manor and Chapel at Whitewell, is probably the work of Walter Urswyk, Chief Forester of Bolland from 1372 to 1413.

LEAGRIM PARK.

(Translated from the Accounts of the Master Forester of Bolland, 1322).

Paid to Adam de Swynhilhurst and Thomas de Crumbilholme (N.B. Both these names are names of farms around Browsholme, and we see very vividly how some local families received their names) for the upkeep of the paling around Laythegryme park both with old and new pales, shores, and rails, from the materials of the King by an agreement for the whole made by the Seneschal . . . 46s8d.

- Paid to the same Adam for upkeep of the New Launde below Fence in Bouland close to the Knottes by agreement for the whole made by the Seneschal . . . 3s3d.

(Knot End is a farm name here. It is not a reference to the great Bolland Knotts in the north.)

- For parchments bought for the Rolls and extracts of the office yearly 2s6d.

- Paid for obtaining 300 rails for the repair of the Launde in Laythgrime park, 100 at 12d . . . 3s.

- For carriage of same, 100 at 12d . . . 3s.

- Paid to a certain carpenter for work on the said rails and posting other old posts and rails around the said Launde for 30 days at 4d a day . . . 10s.

- Paid to certain carpenter for repairing the houses of the Lodge at Laythegrime for two days at 4d a day . . . 8d.

(The Lodge is a reference to the Keeper's house where the Hall now stands.)

[1] Whitaker, i, 352. Very properly the slate-man is called Richard Sclater.

- Paid for repairing the walls of the said houses and for dawbing, two days at 4d a day . . . 8d.

- Paid to a certain roof-maker for roofing and covering the said houses for 10 days at 4d a day . . . 3s4d.

ACCOUNTS OF 1335.

Three items are of special interest :

- Paid for making a gate on the north side of the park by an agreement for the whole made by the Seneschal . . . 2s.

- Custody of the paling of the park. Wage for Nicholas Swynhilhurst working there felling and splitting oaks for the pales and rails, and making one hundred and a half of pales, at 12d per hundred . . . 18d.

- Paid to Henry Pemberton for making 67 roods of new ditch, 8ft. wide, 4½ft. deep, planted with white thorns in 3 rows, on the north of the park.

(The first item gives us the exact date of the making of Park Gate on the north side of Leagrim, where a farm still bears the name to this day.

The second item lets us know that the fence or pale around the park was good, strong oak.

Items like the third are found in the following accounts.)

ACCOUNTS OF 1340.

CUSTODY OF THE FOSSE AT LATHEGRYME.

- Paid to Richard Merseden and his mates working on the making of 160 roods of new Ditch around the park, 8ft. wide and 4½ft. deep, and planted with white thorns in 3 rows, receiving for each rood 8d . . . 106s 8d.

- Paid to Edward Crumbelholme for making 160 roods of paling, placed above the said Foss (Ditch) both with old and new pales, at 2d a rood . . . 26s 8d.

CUSTODY OF THE LAUNDE INSIDE THE SAME PARK.

- Paid to Edward Crumbelholme for felling 60 palesbord for mending the pailing of the Launde in the park there, for the whole 6d.

- For the wage of the said Edward making pynnes for the same, one day's work . . . 4d.

- Paid to Alexander Huntyngden for carrying the said palesbordes, for the whole 6d.

- Paid to Richard Boys working on the making of the railings round the said Launde for 10 days, taking 4d a day . . 3s 4d.

(From the above accounts the reader may easily build up a picture for himself of the workmen felling the oak-trees for the paling or fence on top of the outer ditch, and of the digging out of a trench to the depth of 4½ feet and with a breadth of 8 feet. The outer slope, planted with three sets of hawthorns, and its fence of oak-boards, must have presented a real obstacle to the deer.)

FROM THE ACCOUNTS OF 1457.

Under *Repairs*, a reference to the renovation of a tenement called Wyndeshilles . . . 13s 4d.[1]

(This form of the name now Windy Hills above Chipping is what the student of names would expect in an old name of this type. The North has many *shields* among its old country names, most famous of which are North and South Shields, generally derived from an English word meaning a shepherd's hut or a shed —Middle English *schele.*)

There are similar documents to the above on expenses at Radholme, but as they merely repeat the same sort of information as the above texts about Leagrim, they are not translated. Some of the passages about Whitewell will be found in the account of the Bolland chapels.

In some of the above accounts a rood or rod is mentioned as a measure of length. According to Mr. Fred Wood of Wodehouse, Slaidburn, the old dry-wallers of Bolland used to reckon a rood as seven yards.

A fine view of the Trough looking south. No better example of a trough-like valley could be found.

[1] For the above Leagrim documents see Whitaker, i, 347-349.

CHAPTER VI.

FOREST DWELLERS IN 1323 AND 1341.

One very early record takes us back to the 17th and 18th years of King Edward II, namely 1323-1324. This has been already printed, but some extracts are worth setting down for the benefit of those who would find it difficult to consult the original publication.[1]

FARM OF THE VACCARIES OF BOULAND (Stock-raising Farms.)

William de Gradale for vaccary of Brenand	30s
William de Swynelhurst for a vaccary there	20s
Adam Langto for Whitlidale	30s
The herbage of a place called Whitwalle	12d
Adam de Whitlidale for le Trogh	6s 8d
The same Adam for Glastirdale	6s 8d
Thmas de Bradeley for Heghok	20s
Adam de Gradale for Randolfboth	26s 8d
Adam, reeve of Slayteburne for Netlikar	10s

The extract from the oldest records of Bolland which we have printed above is very valuable indeed as it takes us back to a distant past when we know very little about the dwellers in Bolland. The deed is so old that it belongs to a time when family names were only beginning to become fixed.

The document tells us a great deal if we stop to analyse it. First, let us note that the tenants are called by their Christian name and generally by a place-name that belongs to Bolland, thus we have William de Gradale (Graddell Moor near Croasdale) or William de Swynelhurst. Secondly, let us take note that Adam seems to have been a very popular name for men, four out of seven being so named, although it is possible that Adam Langto is the same person as Adam de Whitlidale.

This early mention of Netlikar, later often called Nettle Carr or Nether Carr, probably shows that the original form was Nettley Carr.

Where was Glastirdale ? It is often referred to in the account-books together with the Trough farm. The Trough farm would

[1] Printed in vol. 41 (1901) Record Society, edited by William Farrar : Some Court Rolls, etc., of Thomas, Earl of Lancaster, in the county of Lancaster.

no doubt be Sykes in the middle of the Trough and Glastirdale must have been somewhere nearby. Today a brook called Lasterdale flows past Sykes.

FOREST DWELLERS IN 1341.

From the accounts of John de Radeclif, Keeper of Clitheroe Castle in the year 1341-1342 we receive some information about the tenants of the royal forest of Bolland at that time. The first part of the record gives chiefly the names of the old farms, but some family names occur later. The rent is described curiously as the sale of grass for stock—"received of the herbage of the vachery of Brenand 46s.8d." The bigger farms are described as a vachery or stock-rearing farm (from the Latin word *vacca*, a cow).

We will now follow John de Radeclif's list :—

Brenand—46s.8d. Swinelhurst—30s
Trogh and Glasterdale—46s.8d. Heghokes—30s
Whitewell—12d. Birkholme (Burholme)—24s.8d.
Broghesholme (Browsholme)—53s.4d. Randolfbooth—46s.8d.

The list now deals with winter and summer agistment of cattle or the sale of wood and turf :—

Received of the winter agistment in the ward of Slaitolm 2s.2d. and summer agistment 3s.3d. Old wood sold there 4s.3d. Agistment at Harop—7s.10d. Bacsholt 8s. for the summer but nothing for the winter because no beasts found there.

The Bashall entry above suggests that a forest officer went round collecting agistment rents from the people who grazed their beasts. The next entries about Bashall are also unusual and worth notice. The wood bought by a forge or smithy there brought in as much money as one of the bigger farms.

Old wood sold (Bashall) 18d. Turbary or turf—3d.

Old wood sold there at one forge by 23 weeks, the week 12d. —23s.

Old wood sold in the ward of Chipin (N.B. the oldest and best form of this village name) 5s.4d.

Agistment of beasts in Radhom Park—£7.0.2d.—a very high rent showing that Radom pasture must have been rich. Old wood sold at Radhom 7s.6d.

Richard de Spaldington for one waste plot in the same chace called Laithgrun (Leagrim)—40s.

We should note here that the above tenancy throws light on the otherwise mysterious description of a farm in an early document called Spaldingtonmonclose.

Where we now find the extensive and well-cultivated farms of Stakes and the Lees, at this period there was only waste land, as in shown by the following :—

John de Plesington for three waste plots called Crombewalholm, Swaynesholm and les Leghes—27s.4d.

Robert de Yholstones for two waste at Haselumbroke and Laithgrun—33s.4d.

Richard de Hoghton for 60 acres of waste at Chipin—20s. Thomas de Knol for 26 acres of waste there—8s.8d. John de Radeclyf for 60 acres of waste 20s. Nicholas de Brenand for 24 acres of waste 8s. William le Bacster for 40 acres of waste—13s.4d. (in the ward of Bacsholf). Robert Spaldington for 12 acres of waste—4s. John de Baylegh for 60 acres of waste at le Parsuere—20s.

The above name le Parsuere is not easy to read in the old deed and it is certainly not easy to place on the map.

John son of Robt. de Yolstones for 15 acres of waste—5s. Adam son of Wm. de Yolstones for 15 acres of waste—5s. Adam de Swinelhurste for 10 acres of waste—3s.4d.

* * *

A later part of the same document describes various expenses, chiefly for the repair of property. The accounts show how low were wages in the terms of modern money, as the following example will show :

And in wages of one carpenter cutting timber in the wood for 12 shed posts, 8 planks for a shed, 40 beams and other timber necessary for repairing the cowhouse at the vachery of Stapelok, and for repairing the aforesaid house upon the plot by agreement 2s.6d.; and in carriage of the said timber 6d.; and in rushes, cut, collected and carried, and roofing the said house 12d. (The above is taken from a Latin document in the Public Record Office, Minister's Accounts—S.C. 6/1091/6).

THE FOREST IN THE YEAR 1464 AND LATER.

The accounts of Sir Thomas Stanley, who was King's Receiver in the fourth year of the reign of King Edward IV—1464-1465—give us a glimpse of how the Forest was farmed out in that distant century. The names of the King's tenants give us useful information about some of the old Bolland families.

To the student of the old records of the Forest through the various centuries it is a matter of no little interest to trace in outline some of the story of old Bolland family names. The more familiar the reader becomes with the old records and the more years he covers in his survey, the more will certain family names stand out as belonging for generations unknown to the soil of Bolland.

The following notes are taken from the old Latin of Thomas Stanley's accounts.

Robert Harreson for Hareden vaccary pays 112s.4d. Agnes Parker for Lykehurst vaccary pays 63s.2d. and for Brentslak (Burnslack) 20s.8d.
John Parker for vaccary of Graystonlegh pays 66s.8d. John Swynelhurste for the vaccary of Fairdakhouse 64s.6d.
Richard Blesdale for Asshknottes and Dynkley Grene 64s.10d.
Henry Merton for vaccary of Stapuloke 60s.4d.
Nicholas Turner for Thorneholme 10s.8d.
John Herryson for half the vaccary of Batherax 63s.4d.
John Herryson for the other half of the same 63s.4d.
John Swynelehurst for half of Bireholme 62s.10d. Nicholas Bounde for the other half of the same 62s.10d.
Richard Parker for two parts of Broghezholme 65s.6d. John Parker for the third part of the same 33s.
Thomas Bounde for the vaccary of Trogh and Sikes 106s.8d.
Nicholas Swynlehurst for the Legh 27s.
Peter Talbot for the third part of Harrop and Netilcarr 21s.2d.
Egidius Talbotte for two parts of the same 42s.2d.

We can see from the above list of families how few were the dwellers in Bolland at this time. The names Parker, Harrison, Bleasdale, Swindlehurst, and Bond are among the oldest and most enduring of Bolland names. The Talbots no doubt belonged to the family of the Talbots of Bashall.

The same document records that John Hoggekynson paid 14s. for Crossedale. This family name occurs for many generations in connection with Crosedale and the upper Hodder.

The account also mentions that Robert Hoghton paid for Lathegryme (Leagrim) £13.6.8., and also paid rent for Accornehurste, Wyndehulles, and Chepenbroke.

It is a pity that we do not know the names of tenants who would sublet from Robert de Hoghton. In the same way we must regret that no tenants' names are given for the lands farmed by James Harrington, one of the important Hornby manor family.

James Harrington knight, paid £30.16s.8d. for various farms and £7.2s. for the Fence. The Fence estate must have included most of the land on the right bank of the Hodder between Dunsop and Whitewell.

The Harrington family must have extended their influence considerably in the Hodder valley during the reign of Edward IV, because this King granted the park of Raddom to Robert Harrington.

What used to be a famous landmark in Bolland—the Harrington Dike, marking the division between Hornby and Bolland—is treated elsewhere.

The document passes to the lands beyond Slaidburn and reverts again to Harrop, as though an item had been forgotten.

"John Hoggekynson for Crossedale—14s.

Sir James Harryngton for certain vaccaries there £30.16.8. and from the same for the Fence . . . 66s.8d.

Egidius Talbot for Harropscore . . . 6s.8d."

The Hodgkinson family were important in Crosdale a century later.

* * * *

The beginning of the reign of Henry VII in 1485 saw the rise to power of Edward Stanley, who became Master Forester of Bolland and lessee of much property. A Christopher Parker was his chief agent in the district. A document mentions Christopher Parker as a servant of Sir Edward Stanley (Duchy of Lanc. Miscellany, xxix, 10, m.17) while others mention him as a joint lessee —e.g. lease of the cornmill and fulling mill at Slaidburn and the corn mill of Bradford for 20 years, lease of the Fence for 20 years. (Duchy of Lanc. Chancery Rolls, Henry VII).

In the year 1502 Sir Edward Stanley obtained a lease for 20 years of most of the Bolland pastures, as follows : Hareden - Likehurst - Brentslake - Gregestonlegh - Faldokeholme - Assheknotte and Dynkley Grene - Stapullok - Turnholme - Betherax - Byrholme - Brokholmes (Browsholme) - Trough and Sykes - Harrop and Ferickarre - Outhed pasture - Park of Laythegrym - Park of

Accornehurst - Windhylles - Pasture near Chepynbroke - Crosedale - Places where Sir Edward was tenant, worth £30.16.8 a year - Fence - A piece of land called Harescroft.[1]

This list resembles that drawn up nearly forty years previously by Thomas Stanley, and the rents are similar, for example the rent for the Fence pasture was 6s.8d. in both cases. The land for which over £30 was paid had been held previously at the same rent by Sir James Harrington ; it was Radholme and its surrounding lands. Although it is not mentioned by name in the deed, an endorsement mentions : Whitladale and Brenand, Radom, le Liez (Lees) with Swynehurst Wardelegh, Gradale and Hokehill alias Highoke, Newhey and Stodehay alias Stodeclose (Hodder Bank today).

We know from a later document belonging to the reign of James I, and printed by Gregson in his *Portfolio of Fragments*[2] that Harecroft was otherwise called Grindleton Score. No doubt it is the same place as Harropscore mentioned at the end of the previous document as tenanted by Giles Talbot. It maintained its rent of 6s.8d. for nearly two centuries.

The name Grindleton Score is confirmed by the fact that the people of Grindleton paid rent for a pasture called Harecroft, as can be seen in the Court Rolls of the Honour of Clitheroe (vol. ii, p. 382), for the year 1527.

Another document shortly after the one just studied above reveals that some increases of rent have been made but that the tenants are not always satisfied, as Sir Edward Stanley, master of the game, would not allow them to keep out the deer :—

"On improvements undertaken by Sir Richard Emson and other Commissioners it was promised the tenants and farmers that the deer should be diminished (mynyshed) and also that they should be suffered so to enclose their grounds that the deer might be kept out of them at all times . . . which promises and covenants be not observed . . . Sir Edward Stanley, Master of the game there, would not suffer the said tenants to enclose any piece of the said ground, but that the Red deer and also the fallow deer may have recourse unto the said ground without lett ; nor would not suffer any of the said tenants to drive them out ; and also that no corn can be sown there for their relief, but the deer destroy it ; which caused the said tenants to make exclamations and complaints . . . "

[1] From Duchy of Lancaster, Chancery Rolls, No. 64, Abstract of Leases, Lancs. & Cheshire, Henry VII.

[2] M. Gregson : *Portfolio of Fragments*, 1869, p. 41.

Rents had been raised by nearly fifty per cent., for example : Likehurst, formerly 63s.2d., let to Rd. and Arthur Parker half for 60s., and half for 30s.7d. Gregestonlegh formerly let at 66s.8d., now let to Reynold Parker for £4. Faredokesholme otherwise called Ferrakhous (Farrick today) lately rented at 63s.6d., now let to John Swynehurst and Robt. Swynehurst for £4.10s. Harrop and Netercarre (otherwise Netelcarre) formerly rented at 77s.8d. now granted to John Clough for £6. Lathegryme formerly for herbage and pannage (swine pasturage) worth £13.6s.8d. is now let to Sir Ric. Shirborne for £20 but he will give this up unless the rent is reduced to £16.13s.4d., which he considers dear enough.

The lands that Sir Edward Stanley leased for £30.16s.8d. can now produce £40 a year as Christopher Parker, servant to Sir Edward has offered that sum.[1]

A farrier, probably Mr Turner from Bentham, shoeing '**Darkie**' in the farmyard at Laythams, on the back road between Slaidburn and Newton. The photograph was probably taken in the early 1940s.

[1] Quoted from Duchy of Lancs. Miscell. XXIX, 10, m.16d, 22-23 Henry VII.

CHAPTER VIII.

NOTE ON THE OLDEST FAMILIES OF BOLLAND.

The very early list of families living over six hundred years ago in Bolland, namely the list of 1323-1324, showed that the number of families must have been small. Four farmers called Adam, two called William, and one called Thomas were mentioned. The likeness of their Christian names may suggest that there was some family relationship between them, and in view of the smallness in numbers, coupled with the remoteness of the district, local intermarriage must have been the rule rather than the exception.

From the foregoing documents, a fair idea can be obtained of the principal families living in Bolland at the end of the Middle Ages—Parkers, Harrisons, Swindlehursts, Bonds, and Bleasdales are already prominent and figure often in later records through several generations. The Clitheroe Court Rolls contain a list of tenants in the Forest for 1443, taken before Richard Earl of Sarum and Thomas Urswyk. From the records already studied, it is easy to recognise familiar names of local families and to point out where they were living five hundred years ago.

TENANTS OF THE FOREST (BOLLAND).

John de Harrington, esquire
Peter Talbot
Richard de Hoghton
Henry de Merton
John Swynlehurst
Robert Harrison
John Parker de Broseholme
Thomas Harreson
Richard Blesedale
William Swynlehurst
Richard Bond
Thomas Bond
Alice, who was the wife of Jn. Harreson
Richard Parker
Agnes who was the wife of Jn. Parker
Geoffrey Sotheron
Thomas Holghton, Chepyndale

From this period of over 500 years ago there were several generations of Parkers at Lickhurst, Browsholme and Graystoneley, Swinlehursts at Farrick, Lees, and Burholme, Harrisons at Batterax and Hareden, Bonds at Burholme, Trough and Sikes, and the Bleasdale family at Dinkling Green. The Talbots at Harrop are no doubt only a temporary offshoot of the Talbots of Bashall Hall. The de Hoghton family of Hoghton Tower were at this period interested in Leagrim and the Chipping district.

The Henry de Merton mentioned was at Stapleoak. No doubt his family is represented by the Martons who appear in later Bolland records. Geoffrey Sotheron was probably the ancestor of some Sowthrons of later date.

The Crombleholmes do not appear in these lists, although their name is of Bolland origin. That is probably because they were tenants or servants of the de Hoghtons on the Leagrim estate. From the Act Book of Whalley Abbey we know that they were at Loud Mytham, where they remained for centuries.[1]

The Act Book kept by the monks of Whalley from 1510 to 1538 shows that the old Bolland families mentioned above were still prominent, and were called upon to be jurymen in the church court at Whalley. The very first entry for Bolland gives Thomas Bond, James Bond and Reynold Parker. While it might be tedious and unnecessary to reprint all the Bolland names in the Whalley book, a few specimens from different years should be of interest to the student of Bolland history.

Jurors, 13 April, 1513. Reginald Parker, George Hogekynson, Robert Cloghe, Edmund Parker.

Jurors, 2 March, 1514. Edmund Parker, James Bond, William Blesedale, John Parker.

28 April, 1515. Edmund Parker, John Parker, Robert Swynhilhurst, Matthew Parker.

In this year is also mentioned one interesting name—Giles Habyrtwayte, spelt the following year as Hatherwhete—very interesting specimens of the local name generally written Hawthornthwaite. He was of "Slatburne", and accused with Isabella Bond.

28 May, 1517. Edmund Parker, Reginald Parker of Grastonlee.

21 April, 1518. Edmund Parker, Raffe Dobson, Robert Swynhilhurst, Thomas Birghe, William Blesdale.

At the court held 30 October, 1518, specially to consider a doubtful marriage, the evidence presented is of more than usual interest to Bolland, the evidence being about Matthew Parker of Lickhurst and Agnes Sourbutts. Edmund Parker, Richard Parker, Thomas Bond, John Swynhilhurst, William Blesdale, Ralph Dobson, and Reginald Parker were called as witnesses about the forbidden degree of relationship between the two. On oath they asserted that James Overend, alias Robinson of Bentham, and Agnes,

[1] *Act Book of Whalley*, Chetham Society, New Series, vol. 44.

former wife of John Parker at Lickhurst were brother and sister. The above named James had a son George, who had a daughter Alice, the mother of Agnes Sourbutts. The above named Alice had a son, James Parker, the father of Matthew. This throws an unusual light on family relationships in Bolland about the time of Henry VIII.

14 April, 1519. Edmund Parker, John Swynhilhurst, Brian Parker, Robert Cromblehorne.

Elizabeth, the widow of Jorn Robynson of Newhethe (Newhey) is denounced for declaring she would keep the black fast to get vengeance on Edmund Parker.

14 April, 1520. Thomas Bond, James Bond, Reynold Parker. John Startivant, Thomas Ryder, Thomas Mersden.

27 May, 1522. John Swynlehurst, Matthew Parker, William Blesadale.

8 April, 1523. John Dobson, Thomas Barowe, Reginald Parker, Giles Turner, Thomas Bond.

6 April, 1524. William Blesedale, Edmund Turner, Reginald Sayer, Arthur Parker.

21 April, 1525. Thomas Dobson, William Wever, Thomas Rider, Christopher Bond.

In 1534 there is a mention of Elizabeth Knoll of Wevar Mylne in Bolland. It may have been connected with the Wever family named above. Its exact location is unknown but it was probably on the Leagrim side of Hodder because a Roger Salisbury of Chipping was cited at the same time before the court.

17 April, 1533. George Hodgekinsone, John Blesedale, James Swyndlehurst, John Parker.

9 April, 1534. John ffranklande, Matthew Parker, Reynald Sawer, Robert Belle.

One of the last entries about Bolland in the Whalley Act Book mentions that Reynald Sawer was commanded to go round Whitewell church on two Sundays carrying a candle for adultery with Isabella Hayerst. This was in 1537. (*Acts*, p. 203).

CHAPTER IX.

AN ANCIENT CHRISTIAN RELIC IN BOWLAND.

A CHAPEL IN A LONELY VALLEY IN THE HILLS.

One of the most isolated and lovely valleys of the north country is the Brennand Valley, close to the more famous Trough of Bolland. It is visited by few people—the sheep-farmers, a few shooting gentlemen, some adventurous hikers, and the men who look after Blackburn's water supply, for Blackburn Corporation is the owner of the Brennand Valley. Yet Brennand is a very old name in Bolland history.

Throughout the centuries there has survived the memory of an old place of worship in Brennand, and even today there is a tradition in the valley that in one corner of a meadow there was once a burial ground. The only recorded evidence about Brennand Chapel, which has come down to us from the past, is in a very old description of Blackburnshire. This was written by the monks of Whalley in the time of Abbot John Lyndley, about 1347.

Abbot Lyndley's monks wrote that : "It should be remembered that there was once in Bouland a certain chapel called *Brennand chappelle*, which chapel then belonged to the parish church of Whalley. And because at that time there was no graveyard there, the bodies of the dead from the whole of Bouland Forest were brought to Whalley and buried there, as being then the mother church." There is no other evidence, so far as is known, and when Dr. Whittaker wrote his famous *History of Whalley*, over a hundred years ago, he says that he does not know of any other tradition.

Searching for Clues.

Recently two searchers went exploring in Brennand to see if they could find any trace of the old chapel, which was perhaps only a memory when the monks of Whalley wrote about it nearly six hundred years ago. They had been told that an old barn at Brennand had a plastered wall—perhaps a clue to the old chapel. Search was first made at Brennand higher barn, with the permission of the farmer's wife. No doubt during the war years she would have been very suspicious about the intentions of two strangers. This search drew a blank, and so a request was made, as a last hope, to see the lower barn by the farm. This request was granted, and inside there stood the plastered wall, but unfortunately its appearance seemed to indicate that it was there as an extra protection for the house.

The good farmer's wife seemed disappointed that there was so little to see, and so drew the attention of her visitors to the markings on a stone slab by the farm-house door. Those markings were of the sort that the searchers had been hoping to find. The stone was rough and weather-worn, as it was lying face upwards to the sky. If it has been there long, it must have passed through many storms, and been worn by rain, ice and snow.

A Design with Five Crosses.

At first sight the markings appear to be the common form of the Christian monogram IHS—Greek letters for Jesus, namely JES, although in the time of the monks these letters were taken to be JHS, the name Jesus being often written Jhesus. Then on closer examination the design seemed to make five crosses in a very ingenious way—one large centre cross, and a cross at each of the four corners. The arm of the letter S at the top left-hand corner had been prolonged to make the crosses more obvious.

This was an interesting discovery, because the old altars have five crosses, one in the centre and one at each corner. The Brennand crosses are gathered into a small space at one side of the stone, probably at the place where the chalice was set upon the altar.

In its present state, the stone is broken and mutilated at one end. If the IHS design was originally in the middle of the slab, the original length would be just over five feet. The width is just over two feet, and the thickness is that of an ordinary stone flag.

There is a circular hole not far from the centre of the slab with the remains of lead plumbing around it. Relics of saints were sometimes placed in altar-stones, but they were usually in the centre so that this circular opening was not in the proper position and may have been drilled in the stone at a later date—perhaps to drain away water.

A Strange Place for a Chapel.

What a strange place for a chapel, this lonely valley in the hills ! Why should this spot have been chosen, seemingly the most isolated in all Bolland ? Without evidence nobody would believe that a chapel had existed by this remote sheep-farm.

And yet, if we turn back to those early centuries and remember that the Norman lords had one castle at Clitheroe and another at Lancaster, between which they would travel with horses and pack-animals, we find that Brennand would be a convenient halfway house, especially for those laden or travelling on foot. Perhaps Brennand in those far-off days was busier than it is now and travellers found there a hostel and a shelter during their rough journey, and here the Normans who generally built a chapel by their establishments set up the *Brennand chapelle* mentioned by the monks of Whalley.

As a last item of interest we may mention that the Christian symbol IHS goes back to the very earliest times, but it became more popular after the eleventh century through St. Bernard's devotion to the name Jesus.

EXCAVATIONS STRENGTHEN BURHOLME CHAPEL THEORY.

OUTLINES OF BUILDING FOUND.

The traveller of to-day may be familiar with the 18th century stone bridge across the Hodder at Whitewell, called Burholme Bridge, or he may have seen on the hillside the buildings of Burholme Farm. Only a student of history knows that Burholme was once more than a farm. It was a cluster of dwellings where several families lived as long ago as four or five hundred years.

There is an old tradition in the valley that there was once a chapel at Burholme. This is borne out to some extent by the fact that in St. Hubert's Chapel at Dunsop Bridge is an old stone font bearing a small metal plate indicating that it was found at Burholme.

When Mr. William Haslewood, of Burholme, was recently asked his opinion on the matter he pointed out a place near the farm where he considered lay the ruins of an old building. Mr. A. Garrard, Surveyor General to the Duchy of Lancaster, gave permission for an investigation of the site.

An Experiment.

When digging was begun on September 10th, 1948, it was not with the expectation that anything of value or even of interest might be found. It was just an experiment that might, with luck, produce results.

After several attempts in heaps of sand, a line of stones, of large size and roughly shaped, revealed the foundations of a wall.

More interesting still was the calculation that the wall faced towards the east, so that this might have been the wall of a building that was "oriented" or built to face east like the old churches and chapels.

Later the outlines of other walls were traced, suggesting a building about 28ft. by 18ft. In the middle of the eastern wall there appeared the foundations of some projecting part, about 7ft. long by 1½ft. wide.

A red floor tile of an ancient pattern, similar to some that may be seen at Whalley Abbey, was found on this projection, also parts of others, which seemed to prove that whatever this old building was it had been given an expensive type of flooring.

Last to be turned up were a door-socket in a heavy stone, and a rather massive stone of unusual shape, but carved simply by a skilled hand. By its shape and design it gave the impression of having served at the top of a pillar or arch as a beam-support or corbel. Unfortunately, no more could be excavated.

Was it a Chapel ?

The objects found by digging show that there was an unusual type of building on this site in the Middle Ages, and with the font at St. Hubert's, Dunsop Bridge, they point to the site of an ancient chapel, and to the projection from the eastern wall as the place of an altar.

It should be remembered that the learned Dr. Whitaker, writing his history of Whalley, nearly 150 years ago, put down the following about Burholme : "Not far from Burholme Bridge are the vestiges of another and more ancient place of worship" (vol. I., p. 335)—more ancient than the chapel at Whitewell, which he dated from Henry VII, but which already existed in the reign of King Henry V. (1413-1422).

The late Colonel J. Parker, Bolland's best historian, pointed out that Burholme was the seat of the Forest Woodmote Court before Whitewell. This provides a further indication that before the building of the Manor-house and Chapel of Whitewell, there was a chapel at Burholme before 1400.

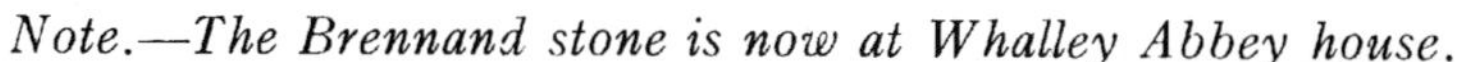

Note.—The Brennand stone is now at Whalley Abbey house.

A favourite picture postcard view of the Trough of Bolland looking north towards Lancaster. How aptly-named **The Wayside Cottage** is.

CHAPTER X.

SOME INCIDENTS IN THE ANCIENT FOREST.

(From documents in the Record Office.)

In 1326, the twentieth year of the reign of King Edward II, Richard de Spaldyngton was made head of the bailiwick of the Royal Chace of Bolland. (Calendar of Patent Rolls, 20 Ed. II m.5). Five years afterwards the townships of Slayteburn, Newton, Grindleton, and Bradford were involved in a lawsuit against the Keepers of Bolland in which Richard de Spaldington gave evidence. He stated that he never levied any but the amount of feeding stuffs and keep (technically called *Puture*) which was formerly levied. He claimed by right of his office to exact this keep (*puture*) in Slaidburn and Grindleton one day each week yearly, except five weeks in Lent, for self and 4 Foresters, 2 lads, 2 dogs, and 1 horse, with a right to 1 bushell of oats and 2 bundles of hay. In Newton there was one *puture* claim 7 times a year, and at Bradford one *puture* each fortnight all the year except in Lent. Richard attended court to make his claim but the tenants of the townships did not appear (Placita coram Rege, 1-22 Edw. III, Hillary anno 5 Ebor. 48).

Elsewhere mention is made of the fact that there were many men called Adam when records were first made about Bolland. Two are mentioned in a tragic affair belonging to the year 1279. Adam of Bolland was taken for the death of Adam of Chapelcroft. He defended himself but was found guilty and hanged. (Assize Roll 1060, Crown Pleas, Trinity 7 Edward I).

About the same time as the previous incident there is a Court record of a suit brought by Adam de Wannervill, Lord of Easington. He was suing about certain tenements in Easington and Bolland against Laurence de Knol, Simon of Clederhowe (Clitheroe), Simon le FitzSweyn, Geoffrey, servant of the parson of Arneclyve, and Walter of Newton. He decided to withdraw his claim and was fined. (Assize Roll 1055, Trinity, 7 Edward I).

There are some other items of interest in the Court records of this same period. John of Easington (Juan of Hesinton) fell from a horse into the Hodder and was drowned. Alexander, his brother, found him ; nobody was thought to blame ; verdict—mischance. The record concludes : "Price of the horse three shillings, for which the Constable of Chester should answer." (Assize Roll 1053, m.5d).

Agnes, daughter of Robert of Boulton, was gathering Bosony (no doubt this should read Bryony or wild vine) in the wood of Bouheland, when a bough fell on her owing to a blast of wind, and crushed her so that she died. The woman who first found her had since died. Judgment—mischance ; price of the bough 5d. The townships of Easington and Grindleton did not come to court and so were fined. The townships of Boulton and Pathorn falsely fixed the value of the said bough, and so were fined. (Assize Roll 1057, Placita Corone, 7 Edw. I., m.4d—Staynecliffe).

We learn from the old records that men of Bolland were among the soldiers who served in France during the long struggle between the English and French kings. In the year 1345, that is in the reign of Edward III, a royal pardon was given at the request of Henry, Duke of Lancaster, to Adam of Dutton of Bakshelf (Bashall) of all felonies and trespasses committed in England before June 16, "on condition that he go when summoned in the King's service to Gascony or elsewhere, and stay at his own charges in such service for a year."

The same pardon was given to Adam, son of John of Croft, John of Wynkedlegh, Elias of Whitlydale, John del Holt of Reuede (Rede?), John son of Simon of Blakey, Laurence son of Richard of Knoll, Robert of Catlowe, Geoffrey, son of Roger of Chadderton, Nicholas of Newhouses of Gradale, William son of Robert of Redecliffe, Richard son of William of Radcliffe, and many others. (Patent Roll, 19 Edw. III. Part 2.m).

Not all the above names are Bolland names, although Whitlydale, Knoll, Catlowe, and Gradale are obviously so. The above document indicates that to gain a king's pardon for some offence, a man could volunteer for a year's service in France. The same sort of recruitment was going on in the century following. In the year 1434, reign of Henry VI, there is a statement about a certain Henry Waddington of Bagsholf, yeoman. "Revocation of the protection for half a year granted to Henry Wadyngton of Bagsholf, yoeman, as about to proceed to France in the company of James Standyssh, esquire ; because he tarries in the said county as the sheriff has testified." (Patent Roll 13 Henry VI, m.28).

Colonel Parker's account of Withgill (see first chapter) mentioned a feud between the Talbots of Bashall and the Singletons of Withgill, and the stabbing of Alice Singleton, in the year 1469. The raid on Bashall Hall was in 1461. It is very likely that these violent disputes were miniature Wars of the Roses, as the nation was passing through that very troubled period.

A similar affair at Skelshaw in Easington was brought before the courts. Stephen Talbot brought a lawsuit against certain people for breaking a close and houses at Scaleshaw in Esyngton and doing damage of £40. The accused were :

Jn Tempest late of Brasewell, knight
Rd Tempest late of Brasewell, Esquire
Thos. Westby late of Holme in Craven yeoman
Thos. Wadyngton of Ydesford yeoman.
Walter Wadyngton of Wadyngton yeoman
Thos. Leyland of Wadyngton yeoman
Jn Perkynson of Esington husbandman
Wm Wadyngton of Thornton in Craven clerk
Rbt. Wadyngton of Cliterhowe yeoman

Staple Oak caught in sunshine by Clitheroe photographer Eddie Pye in the 1930s. The solid-looking house's name may be a reference to the trees found there when Bolland was heavily wooded with English oak.

(Reproduced courtesy of Pye's of Clitheroe)

CHAPTER XI.

HAMERTON.

In spite of having been very much changed and rebuilt, the ancient manor house of the Hamerton family still shows some signs of its former dignity and importance. Both inside and out there are traces of a historic past, and by its very size and proportion the house shows that it was built as a hall and not as a farm-house. One of the most attractive features is a medieval spiral stairway in stone, probably one of the oldest parts of the whole house. In the spacious attics are the great beams set there long ago, but now beginning to feel the weight of years. An enquiring mind might ask why the family that gave the hall its name is now unknown. The shortest answer to that question is—'Pilgrimage of Grace, 1536'.

It was through his share in that protest of the North against the destruction of the monasteries that Sir Stephen Hamerton was attainted of high treason and executed at Tyburn, suffering at the same time at the Abbot of Fountains. Being a knight he was spared the ignominy of drawing and quartering, and was hanged and beheaded—a fate cruel enough. This harsh blow not only ruined the family fortune, but it seems to have killed the will to live in his son Henry, who died on August 4th, 1537, the year of his father's execution. On January 3rd following he was followed by his young wife Joan, leaving two small children, who at the father's death were Margaret, aged one year, and Alice, aged one month. What became of these two girls is not known. An equal mystery covers the fate of the younger daughters of Sir Stephen, Mary and Ann, who are mentioned in the will of their mother Elizabeth. This grief-stricken widow did not long survive the dark tragedy that crushed the head of the Hamerton family and the heir to the estate in the flower of his youth. She was buried at Slaidburn on May 3, 1538. It has been pointed out that it would be considered dangerous to mention the heirs of an attainted subject in any deed, hence the veil of mystery that descends over the fate of these young people.[1]

Those who are familiar with the great tragedies of ancient Greece will remember how the poets trace the terrible working of a dark fate which seems to pursue relentlessly and malignantly first

[1] Details of Henry, Joan and their daughters are in *Escheator's Inquisitions, Series II, File 237, No. 14, York 1 Aug. 30 Hen. VIII.* Inquisition after death of Joan Hamerton, widow. For Elizabeth Hamerton see Whitaker, ii, 517, and Peel, *Knowlmere*, 12. Henry's exact age is in doubt ; he was probably in the early twenties ; his marriage took place some thirty years after that of his parents.

one member of a noble house and then another. The sad fate of the Hamertons may remind us that all in the stories of the Greek poets is not legend or story, but that no doubt there were some grim and awful happenings on which the stories were founded.

The Hamertons had formed close links by friendship and inter-marriage with other notable families that led the Pilgrimage of Grace. Thus Sir Stephen had married Elizabeth, daughter of Sir Ralph Bigod of Settrington, Yorkshire, and their nephew, Sir Francis Bigod, a young man of promise, was executed in 1537 for his part in the Pilgrimage. Incidentally, the Bigod family were descendants of the first Dukes of Norfolk, and this marriage alliance shows the importance of the Hamerton family at this period.

Only a year before the ill-starred Pilgrimage of Grace, Sir Stephen had drawn up a marriage settlement for his son. (8 May, 1535). One of the trustees of this deed is Robert Aske, the famous leader of the Pilgrimage, destined to be executed at York in June, 1537, a victim of Henry VIII's false promises, and a horrible warning to his brethren in the North.

The lady to whom the young Henry Hamerton was married belonged to an ancient and distinguished Yorkshire family, the Stapletons of Wighill. An uncle, William Stapleton, was one of the many Yorkshire gentlemen placed on trial in 1537, and he claimed to have been forced to take part against his better judgment.

Yet another link with a famous Northern family was the wedding of Henry's sister, Margaret, to Sir Walter Strickland of Sizergh, who was 'out' on the Pilgrimage, but afterwards set free. These family ties show what a general movement there was among the landed gentry against the tyranny of Henry VIII.[1]

The only part of the Hamerton estates that was saved from forfeiture to the Crown was the Hellifield estate, which had been settled on Sir Stephen's mother. The extent of the losses suffered may be seen in a document which details what Sir Stephen inherited from his father in 1514 :—the manors of Hamerton, Knolsmere, Wigglesworth, Hellifield, and Langfield, and of the third part of Rishworth, etc., as well as lands in Slaidburn, Newton, Settle, Pheser, Calton, and Coniston Cold. Hamerton and Knollmere were held of the King, as of the Duchy of Lancaster, by fealty and service, at the court of Bolland.[2]

The origins of this family are obscure, but it is possible that they were settled in the valley before the Norman Conquest.

1 Whitaker, ii, 517, Henry's marriage. For Margaret see Peel's Knowlmere, 12, and *History of Stricklands of Sizergh.*

2 Whitaker, ii, 516.

The first of the name to achieve some importance was Stephen, son of Hugh, who witnessed some Pudsay deeds, about the year 1200, and who could afford to give the monks of Kirkstall 20 cartloads of hay a year.[1] Stephen was a favourite name in the Hamerton family, and the memory of this fact survives today in such places as Stephen Park and Stephen Moor.

The gift of Stephen to Kirkstall is only the first of many benefactions of the Hamerton family to the cause of religion. It is probable that Chapelcroft above Newton was part of the endowment of a Hamerton chapel at Slaidburn. The evidence for this is not certain. Chapelcroft existed before 1278 because in that year a certain Adam of Chapelcroft was murdered by Adam of Bouland, who was found guilty and hanged.[2] The evidence for the endowment of a Hamerton chapel in the manor of Hamerton only dates from 1333, but this is not conclusive because the same evidence suggests that the chapel had existed before it was officially endowed and licensed by William Melton, the Archbishop of York.[3] As will be seen from an examination of the list of forfeited property belonging to Sir Stephen Hamerton, printed later in this chapter, the family estates surrounded Chapelcroft from Meaneley on the Easington boundary and then passing towards Foulscales and Knollmere. Chapelcroft must therefore have been carved out of this estate. According to the evidence of a Slaidburn Court Roll for 1589 the farm Long Strypes was originally part of Chapelcroft, and this would seem to indicate that the original Chapelcroft must have formed part of the manor of the Knoll family. No doubt this family first made a church grant from chapel croft or even had a chapel there. Then some time after 1300 when the heiress of the Knoll family, Katherine, married Adam de Hamerton, the Knoll estate passed to the Hamertons. Whereupon Adam's father, Stephen, arranged a larger and more permanent endowment of '36 acres of land and twenty of meadow at Slaiteburn and Newton.'

The Hamertons maintained a strong link with Slaidburn church ever since the time when Fulco, Prior of the Benedictine monastery of Pontefract, granted about the year 1231 Slaidburn parish and its tithes to Stephen de Hamerton, clerk.[4] Two centuries later Lawrence Hamerton began to rebuild Slaidburn church and the work was carried on by his son Richard.

In Colonel Parker's account of the Hamertons the reader may study some examples of the lawlessness common in Bolland about

[1] Whitaker, ii, 515.
[1] Assiz Roll 1060, Crown Pleas Trinity, 7 Edward I, m.l.d.
[3] Whitaker, ii, 518.
[4] Pontefract Chartulary, Fasc. xi, 510.

the time of Edward I or in the years before 1300. He mentions two of the Hamertons outlawed in a murder case, basing his statements on a series of extracts from the Court trials. There are other examples. 'John, son of Adam of Hamerton, and Edmund his brother met Gilbert, son of John Stelying of Horton, and strife arose, and John struck Gilbert on the head with a fork and Gilbert died. John fled.[1] About the same time 'Nicholas of Hamerton was taken for robbery at Hamerton, and taken by the vills of Sleteburn, Essyngton, and Newton, towards York prison, and Henry of Blakeburn, Forester of Penhill, took him at Bradford Bridge from the said vills, conducted him into Lancashire and there he was beheaded.'[2]

The student of medieval history, especially of North country history, is not surprised to find evidence of raiding, fighting, and physical violence, which were even more common towards the Border than in Lancashire and Yorkshire.

No doubt the family combined a rugged and sturdy independence of character, together with a sincere attachment to their religious faith, so that it is little surprising that they should have joined in such a cause as the Pilgrimage of Grace.

The following is a list of the forfeited possessions of Sir Stephen. It is most valuable for the names of people and of places living just over four hundred years ago.

September 29, 1537. Rents of all tenants at will to be paid equally on the feast of St. Martin and Whitsun . . . . total of £74.13.4. in Bolland.

- of John Bonde for 1 messuage called Brokthorne with a garden and 20 acres pasture	1	6	8
- of Thomas Place for a house with garden called Brookhouse Greene and 15 acres meadow and pasture	1	6	8
- of the relict of the late G. Parker for a house with garden called Stevyn Park, 4 acres arable, 5 acres meadow, 40 acres pasture and moss	4	13	4
- of Thomas Hatecole (Hatkill) a house with garden called Staynrays, 3 acres arable, 2 meadow, 2 pasture	2	3	4
- of George Holden 1 messuage with garthon called Rayngill, 4 acres arable, 6 meadow, 6 pasture	3	13	4
- of Wm. Cayley for ½ messuage called Blakhouse with garthon, 2 acres arable, 4 meadow, 4 pasture	1	16	8

[1] 22 Edward I, Assize Roll, 1101, m.51.

[2] As above, m.54.

- Thos. Marton for other ½ with garthon, 2 acres arable, 4 meadow, 4 pasture	1	16	8
- of Robt. Parkinson 1 house with garden there called Fynnesse, 2 acres arable, 4 meadow, 2 pasture	2	0	0
- Rd. Hamerton 1 house with garton, 3 acres arable, 4 meadow, 4 pasture	3	6	8
- of Roger Stowte 1 house with garton called Byg-house, 3 acres arable, 4 meadow, 6 pasture	2	13	4
- and of £1.4.8 of total rents of tenants at will of the Lord in Woodhouse :			
of Robt. Standen for 1 house 8 acres arb. mead. past.		10	0
Relict of Rd. Browne for 1 house called Brakenhall 8 acres		8	0
- of John Steward 1 house with garton, 3 acres		6	8
Total	25	18	0

Rent of Mill. 10s. for rent of Corn Mill on the water called Hodder held by Eliz. Hamerton, widow, paid yearly at St. Martin and at Whitsun.
Rent of Manor. £13.6.8. from rent of Manor of Hamerton with appurtenances, and 6 acres arable, 12 meadow, 40 pasture, held by Lady Eliz. Hamerton, widow.

MANOR OF KNOLLMERE & NEWTON. Rents of tenants at will.

- of Rbt. Parker and Giles Parker for 1 tenement with garthon called Fowlescales, 4 acres abl., 6 mead, 20 past. and wood	4	0	0
- of John Batson for 1 tenement called Yolstanes with garthon, 8 acres mead., 30 past. and wood	3	6	8
- of James Lee for 1 tenement called Byrkhead with garthon 4 acres arable, 6 mead. 20 past. and moss	3	13	4
- of Thomas Burrows for 1 tenement called Mates-hill with garton, 2 acres abl. 1 mead. 3 past.	1	6	4
- of Nich. Turner for 1 tenement called Peverhill or Knollstanes with garton, 3 a.able, 2 mead. 1 past.	1	3	4
- of Ths. Rudd for 1 tenement called Knollhall, with garton, 3 ar. 3 mead. 3 past.	1	13	4
- Jn. Bond 1 tenement called Mossethwaitehouse with garton, 2 acres arable, 3 mead. 8 past.	1	10	0
- of Thos. Turner for 1 tenement called Nether-thorneholm with garton, 1 acre ar. 2 mead. 6 past.	1	10	0

- of Giles Parker for 1 close called Overholme		6	8
- of Jn. Hogekynson for 1 close of past. called Asshenhyrsthey	2	3	4
- of the relict of the late Jn. Langshaw for 1 tenement called Knotthouse with garton, 2 acres ar. 1 mead.		7	0
- of the relict of Patrick Ranguill for 1 tenement called Whitehawehouse with garton, 2 acres ar. 1 mead. 1 small croft		15	0
- of Christopher Ranguill for 1 tenement called Orchinstrett with garton, 3 acres ar. and mead. and small croft called the Fall		8	0
- of the relict of Rd. Parkynson for 1 tenement called the Moldeholles with garton, 2 acres ar. 1 mead. and 1 little croft called the Overparock		9	0
- of Thos. Parker for 1 tenement called Hyndegyllhouse with garton, 1 acre mead. and 1 past.		9	0
- and of 50s. of total rent of tenants at will in Newton :			
- of Roger Proctor and Jn. Proctor for 1 tenement with garton in Newton, 3 acres ar. 2 mead. and 1 little croft by estimation 1 acre		16	8
- of Jn. Stakehouse for 1 tenement called Menelay with 1 garton and 13 acres ar. mead. and past.	1	0	0
- Thos. Lee for 1 house with garton there, 2 acres ar. 2 mead. and 1 little croft called the Fall by estim. 1 ac.		13	4

(From Duchy of Lancaster. Minister's Accounts. Henry VIII no. 4356.)

Two names in the above list are worth noting. There is the farm in Knollmere called Yolstanes. This is a name which has now disappeared from the district, although it probably survives in a name written on the map as Bonstone. It is mentioned next after Folescales in this record and in another document quoted elsewhere, so that it may have been what is now called Gibbs, lying behind Folescales towards Bonstone wood. In the records of Slaidburn court Yolstonewood seems to have been a name for an area where there were several holdings.

A second name of interest is that of James Lee of Birkhead or Birkett. He is no doubt the remote ancester of the J. Leigh of Marl Hill or Birkett who built a chapel at Newton in 1696.

The Mateshill is probably represented on the modern map by Matril Laithe near Knowlmere. Knollstones was below Boasden, as also Knollhall, which should be written Knollhaw.

Overholme is no doubt Higher Thorneholme, being one of the easier names on the list. Many of the later names are hard to identify.

According to Miss Peel, in 1805 the farm now called Moor End, near Oxenhurst, was called the White House. This may be the Whitehawehouse. In which case, Knott house will be somewhere near the Knott or Sugar Loaf Hill, and Asshenhyrsthey may be the Hey above Oxenhurst.[1]

Following Miss Peel again, the farm of Hung Hill near Boasden now has enclosed with it the land of Lower Staynes and of Mould Hill, whose buildings have disappeared. No doubt this Mould Hill is the Moldeholles of the Henry VIII record.[2]

Colonel Parker's account of Hamerton tells how it passed from one family to another. In 1545 it was granted by Henry VIII to Ralph Greenacres for a knight's service, which meant no doubt a large sum of money. How decadent the idea of a knight's service had become under the Tudors is shown by the fact that in 1555 Greenacres obtained leave to dispose of the manor to Oliver Breres and his heirs.

The Breres family from Preston were connected with the Tempests of Catlow and with the Guys of Halstead. Lord Farrer, the historian, whose family sprang from Greystonely in Bolland, used to think that one of his family, through a link with the Guys, helped to interest Mr. Humphrey Chetham of Manchester in the purchase of Hamerton Hall. The Chetham charity held it until very recently, when it was bought by Mr. C. King-Wilkinson.

In conclusion the following quotation of an Assize Roll of the year 1267, in a suit against Stephen de Hamerton by William de Tabellay, may be given for sake of the names of the sureties.

"Sureties for Stephen—Benedict of Slaynemere
Ralph Cotes of Newton
Geoffrey of Menley of Newton
Wm. Malasise of Bolton

Sureties for William—Luvecok Othepectesand
Boteman his brother
William of Knol of Waddington
Henry Bot of Bascheshelf . . . ."[3]

[1] Peel, *Knowlmere*, p. 44.

[2] The same.

[3] Assize Roll 1050, Hilary, 52 Henry III, m.31.

Note that Stephen's names belong to Newton and that Slaynemere is probably the oldest form of the name Slim Row, which used to be written Slanemorrow. Othepectesand is an extraordinary name.

In writing this chapter on the story of the Hamertons and their part in the Pilgrimage of Grace, the authors have felt that this was the one part of their story of purely local facts and persons which merged and became one with the great stream of the national history. The Hamerton story is only a small part of the history of the Pilgrimage of Grace, nevertheless the pages here written approach the subject from a new and unusual side, so that through the familiar detail of local history with its story of family weddings and blood connections, the reader grasps perhaps more than in the pages of a greater history something of the movement of the clans of Northern England, rising against the avarice and despotism ot Henry VIII.

Some of, or perhaps all, the pupils of Newton School about 1910. Behind the kneeling boy is young Joe Frankland, whose father farmed in the village.

CHAPTER XII.

CROSDALE.

The modern traveller along the lonely and boggy road from Slaidburn to Hornby, as he passes through the wild and severe beauty of Crosdale valley, may well marvel at the fact that the Romans made a road across this difficult country. Today some of the local farmers, who know these fells from long experience, disagree about the direction of the Roman road, but there is every likelihood that it continued more or less on the track of the modern road until it passed Sandy Gutter, when it struck across Botton Head Fell in a north-easterly direction. The line of the road is clearly traced between Newton and Woodhouse, and again over Botton Head.

Crosdale is most frequently mentioned in old documents with regard to boundaries. Thus one of the earliest references is by the monks of Kirkstall ; their Latin reads as follows : "The bounds between Gradal and Crosdale begin at Wyndyhates, and so to the Slaytbrok, and thence to Berkslacheyd, and so to the Bulstanis, and then to Crosdalheyd. Gradall from Crosdall to Hoder, and Crosdale goes as far as Wytlyngdall."[1]

This old document is full of interest, as it suggests that the old name of Crosdale brook is Slaytbrook, from which Slaidburn no doubt takes its name ; it also explains the origin of Whitendale, namely the dale of the white ling. A name like Berkslacheyd is unknown in the valley today, although from other documents it appears to have been between Crosdale and Whitendale. A name like Birkslackhead would suggest a slope with birch trees, but there are no trees today.

A certain number of documents about Crosdale have come down from the reign of Queen Elizabeth. In the sixteenth century the pasturage of Crosdale was for a long time farmed out to members of the Hodgkinson family, and in 1575 Utride Hodgkinson[2] was in legal dispute with some of the farmers of Slaidburn about their rights to common pasture between Crosdale and Hodder. This area is always called Rawmoor in ancient documents, and at one time it must have covered a very large acreage. Today very few dwellers in the district have ever heard of Rawmoor, and it was only after long searching enquiry that a young farmer at Merrybent pointed out that lands below Merrybent towards the Hodder are still called Rawmoor. A very shrunken Rawmoor that must be, seeing that the old deeds let us know that it extended into the hills by Hare Clough Head, and seventeenth-century improvements at

[1] *Kirkstall Cartulary*, ccccxxiii.

[2] A similar dispute took place 25 years before, for which see County Records, Preston—Dispute between King's tenants at Slaidburn and John Hogekynson concerning pasturage of Croyssdale Score, 1549/50.

Round Hill not far from Crosdale were called improvements on Rawmoor.[1]

Utride Hodgkinson was clearly attempting to restrict the common grazing rights near Crosdale, and to do this he appears to have used several methods. First he claims rights on a tongue of land extending from Crosdale and Hare Clough Head towards Hollins in the direction of the Hodder, thus cutting into the old common pasture of Gradel and Rawmoor. He advances as an argument that his father John was paid for the 'gyste' of sheep and cattle "by the Cross Bank and the Reed Skye towards the Hollins". A final argument put forward is that the tenants of Slaidburn have enough common pasture on Champion—an argument which rather betrays the fact that Utride Hodgkinson was uneasy about his right to these lands, and in fact the farmers who gave evidence denied that Champion was enough for summer grazing.

The records of this dispute are chiefly valuable for the preservation of old names and landmarks, many of which have now been completely forgotten. Captain F. Mitchell, who possessed a copy of some of the evidence in this dispute, made a great effort to identify some of the places named and was helped by some of the men who had farmed the district for years, and yet many of the landmarks remained unidentified. The present authors fared little better until they tried detective work on the old records, comparing names there with names or fragments of names on the six-inch maps. Thus Cross Bank Laithe gave a clue to Cross Bank Foot of 1575, and a Chancer Nook nearby suggested Charneshaye of 1575.

The following are some of the chief landmarks for the bounds of Crosdale as put forward on July 27, 1575 at Rishton Grange before Sir Richard Shireburn, Ralph Assheton and Alexander Rigby. Begin at the gray stone in Pykell Dike, ascending something N.W. to Reed Syke Foot, and so ascending Cross Bank Foot N.W., then to the great stone in the graines of Charneshay, and from thence over the hill to the gray stone in the side of Wynde Yates, and from thence to the low Standeres. From the gray stone in Crosedayle beneath Dry Clough Foot west to Dry Clough Head, west up the Rigg as heaven water comes, inward, to Crosedayle to a great stone in the head of Hynde Slack and then over the height to the Tarn of Blabro Fell, then north to the Black Brook Head as heaven water comes, over Blackstone Fell to Shoter Clough Head as heaven water . . . . , to Myrke Slack Head as heaven water . . . , to Takerdowne Lache in Crosedayle Head, thence to the east end of Whitledale, Bullstone, the east end of Botton Crag, eastward to Whitle Hill, to Fakermore Slack as heaven water comes from Hare Clough Head into Crosedayle, southward to the Stubb Cross short of Gradell Dyke Nook on the

[1] For the following paragraphs please consult the Crosdale map.

head of Rawmoore, and by Whippe Clowe Head to the great stone in Pykell Dike first mentioned.

The Wynde Yates mentioned above was stated by the monks of Kirkstall to lie at the beginning of the bounds between Gradel and Crosdale. If we go from Charnshay over the hill in a westerly direction. an old road leads us to a place called 'Clough' at the top of Moor Syke and about half-way between Fell Side and Croasdale House. There is little doubt that this used to be Windyates, and in fact the boundary line today passes on the hill above this to the Dry Clough by Crosdale brook.

The Blabro or Blaber Tarn is mentioned more than once, but though its site is known, it does not exist at the present time. Blackstone Fell is described on the map as Baxton Fell. No doubt Myrke Slack Head is the Birk Slack Head of the Kirkstall deed.

Facker Moor is probably a mistake for Thacker Moor, which is known today as a place for gathering rushes for thack or thatch. Some of the evidence in a document quoted later mentions the gathering of rushes for "thacke".

It would be a thrill to discover the "Stubbe Cross short of Gradell Dyke Nook on the head of Rawmoor." However, there is little doubt about where it stood. Gradell Dyke comes down the slope above Merrybent Farm, which must at one time have been in the middle of Rawmoor. The Stub Cross would be at the top of the slope where the hill begins to climb to Hare Clough Head.

The name of Graddell Moor, which occurs so often in old documents, is generally unknown today. After a long and fruitless quest for it, the present writers found that it lay above Merrybent from Mr. George Strickland of Slaidburn, an old country craftsman that it was a pleasure to meet.

Various items of interest from the depositions taken at Slaidburn in 1550 may be quoted for the sake of record. One of the witnesses was Thomas Tunstall, priest, aged 50, one of the King's tenants of Slaidburn, affirmed that the tenants of Slatburne and the house called the Hollyns and the house called Fennyis had for the last 25 years right of pasturing, with common rights of turf and thatch on Crosdale Score.

Robert Hyde, priest, aged 57, of Slaidburn, affirmed that this right had held for 40 years.

John Haslett of Slaidburn bore witness like the said Thomas Tunstall except that the right had been held for 60 years. The witness was age 72.

Other witnesses were Robert Bond of Saykes in Bolland, John Robinson of Brennand, William Banster, gentleman, Thomas Browne of Whyttleden, George Holden, John Banke of Slaidburn aged 80, John Toller aged 74, Robert Chapmon, John Hanson.

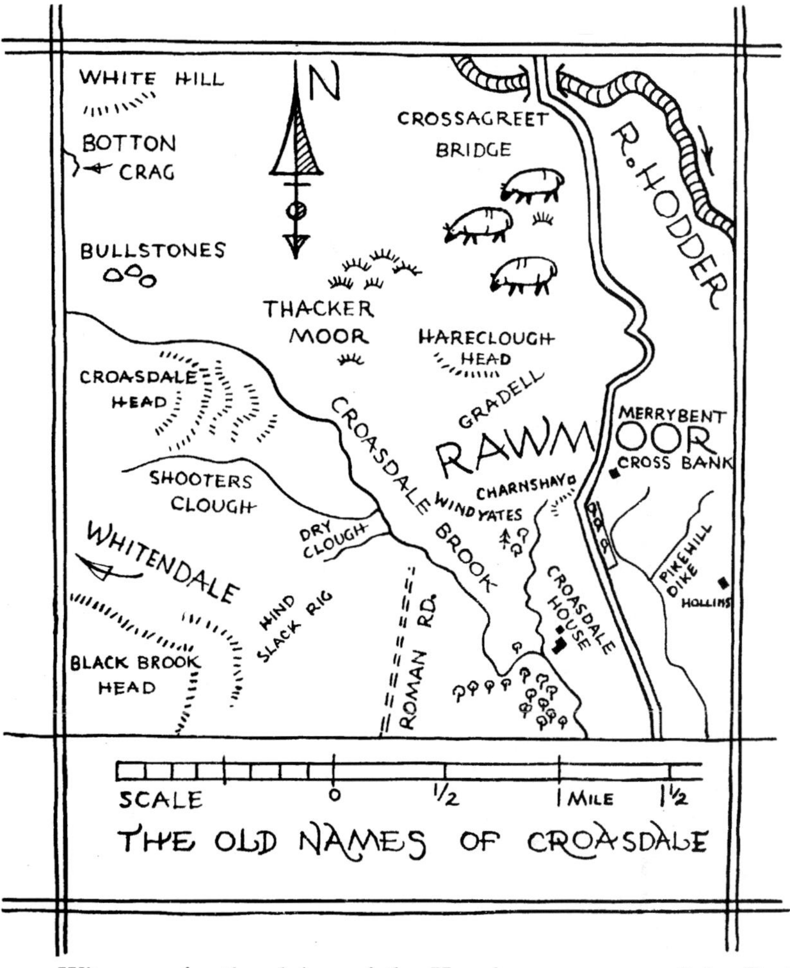

Witnesses for the claims of the Hogekynsons were : John Parker of the Highefield, Christ. Brenand of the Highfield, John Eskholme of Woodhouse, and John Cloghe of Grindleton testified about his father at Woodhouse.[1]

A quotation has already been made from the evidence taken at Rishton Grange (now under the water) in July 1575 when the dispute about Crosdale was continued before the Royal Commission. Most of the evidence at this date backs up the claim of Utride Hogekinson to demand rent for "Gyste" of sheep and cattle upon the Reed Syke, the Cross Bank, and so to the Hollins, thus limiting the rights of the Slaidburn tenants upon Rawmoor.

The chief witnesses were Robert Parker of Harden, aged 62, Utride Hogekynson of Shawe House in Slaidburn, Christ. Coate of

[1] Document at Preston.

Haskell Clough, aged 66, Christ. Brockeden of Rishton Mere, aged 30, Richard Holden of Rishton Mere, aged 47, Edward Banke of Rishton Mere, aged 55.

The most outstanding piece of evidence was offered by the above Christopher Coate, who referred to an affray between Richard Hamerton, esquire, and his servants when challenged by John Hogekynson about forty years before (1535). Hamerton came into Crosdale at a place called Charne Shaw to take away rushes and bent for thacke, which his men had cut down "near unto the gray stone in the side of Wyndeyates and the Low Staneres". "The said John did not only stay the said Hamerton and his servants from carrying away the same, but also did make an affray at the same time upon the said Hamerton and his servants, whereupon the said Hogekinson did shoot an arrow into the shoulder of the said Hamerton's horse, whereupon they departed without carrying any thacke away."

Another document that has survived from this Elizabethan age contains eight lists of sheep and cattle in Crosdale from 1576 to 1582. Unfortunately, we can do no more than mention its existence in case some reader might wish to refer to it.[1]

To the middle of the next century belongs a more interesting document, which contains an order by George Pigott, Steward of the Manor of Slaidburn to Christopher Parkinson, deputy-bailiff, to put John and Charles Nowell, Gentlemen, in possession of "Croasdell House" and specified closes, dated 1651. The Nowells were for several centuries a well-known family in the Hodder valley, and there are still some living who bear the name. A reference in this same document to a certain house "called Hill House" is very likely an indication that what is now called "House of Croasdale" was then called Hill House.

As a conclusion to these notes on Crosdale a list has been compiled of some of the chief families of this district of Crosdale and Rawmoor before 1800 in the hope that it might be of interest to some present representatives of these old families. It may be noted in passing that the seventeenth century seems to provide more family names than any other. Probably in the eighteenth century many people had already begun to move towards the new industrial areas.

FAMILIES IN CROSDALE AND RAWMOOR.

Before 1600

1550 John Banke
Robert Chapman
Christopher Hogekynson
John Hogekynson
Richard Hogekynson
George Holden
John Toller

[1] See list at end of chapter.

1575 Cristopher Atkinson
Edward Bank of Rissheton Meyre
Christopher Brockeden of Rissheton Meyre
Christopher Coate of Haskell Cloughe
John Coate of Graddilk (Gradel)
Thomas Coulthurst
Utride Hodgkinson
Richard Holden of Rissheton Meyre
Robert Jackson
Thomas Oain (The Wain Hill towards Crosdale may bear the name of this family ; in the next centuries the name Windle appears, which may be Wain Hill.)

It is perhaps of interest to note that the name Christopher, which appears several times before 1600, continued for several hundred years to be one of the most popular names for men in this district.

Before 1700

Atkinson
Bayley
Blezard
Brennand
Carr
Coare
Egland
Frankland
Hatkill
Hide
Holden
Hodgkinson
Myres
Pickhaver
Robinson
Spencer
Taylor
Varley
Waddington
Windle

Before 1800

Blageborrow
Brigg
Clapham
Robinson
Rudd
Sharples
Squire
Taylor
Varley
Windle

Names of Farmers sending Sheep to Gist on Crosdale.

1576.

Adam Hatkill
Christopher Bridge
Ric. Stowt
George Bounde
Brian Taylour
John Ellis
Oughtred Hodgkinson
Charles Hodgkinson
John Brennand
Ric. Brennand
Edmund Scott
Thom. Hatkill
George Atkynson
Thomas Hyde
Ric. More
Chris. Bradley
Wilm. Harrison
John Battersby

Rob. Atkinson
Chris. Slynts
Thoms. Banke
John Sygeswike
Ought. Hodgkinson
Edwn. Pymett
Thom. Battersby
Mr. Whies
Mr. Ric. Braddyll
Wm. Jackson
Thom. Brown
George Mytton
John Layte
Jas. Newsham
Wm. Brown

1582.

Oughtred Hodgkinson
Ric. Stowt
Thom. Hyde
Widow Jackson
George Origh (Orreg)
Ric. Hodgkinson
Thos. Brown
John Brennand
Ric. Brennand
Rob. Wilkinson
Wm. Harrison
Nic. Harrison
John Battersby
John Ellis
Christ. Scott
Christ. Bradley
Eliz. Bankes
Christ. Bankes
Christ. Smithson
Ric. Scott
Rob. Hyde
Rob. Brennand
Ric. Woodworth
Ambrose Bolton
Adam Hatkill
Christ. Hodgkinson
Christ. Atkinson

The above names are from list of sheep gisted in Crosdale, now deposited at Preston by Capt. F. Mitchell.

FIELD NAMES OF CROASDELL HOUSE.

Slaidburn Court 1645.

Ralph Walker of Underhill in Yorkshire, gentleman, surrendered tenancy of Croasdell House with a Turfhouse and a barn called Oxbarn and the following lands—Cornhill Sower Ing, the hillwood containing ten and a half acres, also one barn called a Sheephouse, two gardens and closes, following to a certain house called Hillhouse, containing ten and a half acres in Slaidburn Woodhouse, also part of the new improvements on Rawmoor called Oxenhouse, also part of the new improvements on Rawemoor called Roundhill containing 27 acres, and another part called Roundhill Far Ramsclough containing 21 acres and another part called Ramsclough containing 22 acres, and one other close called Stockfield, and one other close called the Hey containing 21 acres.

From a document in Preston Record Office dated 1651 to Christopher Parkinson Deputy Bailiff, authorising possession tc John and Charles Nowell.

CHAPTER XIII.

CHAMPION HILL AND CHAMPION DIKE.

The student of the map of Bolland will notice that part of the high ground between Hodder and Ribble above Slaidburn is called Champion. Several farms have the same name. At first it seems to be an unexpected name to find in this district. That is because it has lost its old meaning. The word derives from ***champagne***—a form of the French word for countryside. The Normans, who of course introduced the word, seem to have used it to imply grazing land. The modern dictionary states that "champaign" means open country. The Champion of Bolland was for centuries waste or common used primarily by the inhabitants of Slaidburn for rough grazing. By old custom the inhabitants of Easington, Holden, Grindleton and Chatburn enjoyed part of the same pasture in the places nearest to their parishes.

Before it was enclosed Champion must have been quite extensive. Even today, when so little unenclosed land is left, there is still a piece of Champion that has never been enclosed or reclaimed by man. It lies near the main road, not far from Greenwood's farm.

One of the old landmarks of Bolland used to be called Champion Dike, and is mentioned in one of the old boundary descriptions (See Chapter on Boundaries). The memory of such a dike has quite perished in Bolland, and nobody either on Champion or near Champion today could give any information about such a dike. Yet it certainly existed, and the present writers believe that after many fruitless journeyings they have discovered the line of it.

The method followed was to pinpoint on the map all references to places near Champion mentioned in the old boundaries. Then to draw a tentative line to mark where the Champion Dike probably ran. The last task that involved many weary miles was to survey this probable line of the Dike on the spot and to see if anything in the countryside and the lie of the land might suggest the old landmark.

There is a very definite man-made ditch that runs from below Harrop Fell close to the roadside, falls into the valley by Lane Ends, and then goes along the side of what would be Champion common in the old days, and continues for a long distance towards Slaidburn. The first part of this ditch would be the Harrop Dike mentioned in the old boundary, and the other part would probably be the old Champion Dike. One of the farmers in the neighbourhood referred to these as Roman Dikes. This may be an indication that their depth, width, and straightness of line has struck some local observers as unusual.

What would be the purpose of those who made Champion Dike ? It would have been cut partly for drainage and partly as a landmark and boundary. In the unenclosed and rough common or waste it would take the place of the modern dry walls and hedges.

Champion in the reign of Elizabeth I.

The Public Record Office has a valuable old document about a Royal Commission on the rights to graze upon Champion. Sir Richard Shireburn, Richard Assheton, John Bradyll, and William Kenyon were appointed Royal Commissioners to inquire into the rights of Slatburne, Grindleton, Holden, Easington, and Chatburne. This was by letter dated May 17th in the ninth year of the reign.

The Commission held its enquiry at Slaidburn on the 29th of May. There was a jury formed of the "most substantiellest and honest men" on the various townships concerned.

Hughtryde Hogekinson Bryan Talbot Robt. Hogekinson Thomas Hyde Wm Cote Wm Brenand	of Slaidburn
Richard Craven Nicholas Standen Gilles Parker	of Esington
Nicholas Robinson Richard Kendall Edmund Dawson John Tayliour	of Chatburne
John Swindlehurst	of Fold
Thomas Waddington Thomas Chapman Robt Woodd Roger Lemynge Thomas Ellis	of Grindleton
Henry Pele Thomas Walcar John Broxhupp Thomas Proud	of Holden

The jurymen testified that the inhabitants of Slaidburn, Grindleton and Esington have had rights of common on Champion without paying. The inhabitants of Holden had rights of

Common for all cattle, paying yearly to the Crown. The inhabitants of Chatburne had common for all "cattels except kyen and yearings", paying yearly three shillings.

Sir Henry Darcy claims that by grant of Robert de Lacy to the Abbey of Sawley (whose rights he had acquired after the dissolution of the monastery) he had all the land called Acreland and the hundred acres of land lying near the 30 acres of land against Caterege, and there pasture for 30 kyen and their increase under 3 years.

The Jury declares that Sir Henry Darcy has the Acreland and that he has the 30 kyen afforesaid enclosed with ditch, hedge and wall, but he has never had any kyen on Champion within memory of man.

As to the further claim of Sir Henry Darcy for right of pasture in the forest between Slaidburn and Bolton in virtue of another deed of the late monastery of Sawley, the Jury deny that such a right was ever exercised. The Abbot, and since the suppression of the monastery the owners and farmers of the property, have been used to put horses and mares and other cattle on Champion because of the demesne lands which they held in Grindleton.

The document goes on to declare that the Commissioners have measured, meared and set forth the said waste ground called Champion as follows :

To the township of Slaidburn 400 acres on the north-west end, set forth by meres and bounds abutting on Stenemore on the north and upon the part of Champion allotted to Grindleton on the east end, and abutting on that part of Champion allotted to Holden and Chatburne on the south, and abutting on Easington in the west.

To the township of Easington 130 acres

To the township of Grindleton 368 acres

To the township of Holden 12 acres

To the township of Chatburn 12 acres, "adjoining to a certain ground called Harroppe."

These meres of Champion, continues the document, being set forth after the rate of seven yards to the pole or rood, and five score to the hundred, there remains of the said Champion 17 acres to be appointed to Chatburn or to Sir Henry Darcy or otherwise among the townships according to their petition.

* * *

In the document studied above we find the old name of Stephen Moor, namely Stenemore. This is a form of the old name that suggests a different meaning from the modern name, probably Stonemoor.

(The document quoted is Duchy of Lancs. Special Commissions, No. 158. Public Record Office.)

CHAPTER XIV.

THE FOREST ABOUT 1550.

Leagrim and Little Bolland were Royal Forest until 1556, and Great Bolland or Yorkshire Bolland until 1662. Because of this fact the Public Record Office possesses quite a number of old documents about Bolland, especially in the Tudor period of the sixteenth century. A few of these documents were printed in Smith's *History of Chipping*. Instead of reprinting these, it has been decided to make extracts from them and to make such notes on them as will link them up with other information about Bolland.

In 1548 we find that Thomas Catterall Esq., John Parker and Elizabeth Parker, widow, had "with bows, arrows, swords, bucklers and other weapons "forcibly kept certain pastures called Whiteladale, Brennand, Lees, Swynlehurst, Wardeleygh, Gradale, New Hey, Stodeley, and the Fence." These were claimed by Ralph Greenacres before the Duchy Court as tenant of Sir Arthur Darcy, Master Forester (1543-1550). Elizabeth Parker admits that she was tenant at will of Swinhillhurst Ing under Sir Arthur Darcy and has since given up possession.

Greenacres and Sir Arthur Darcy were landowners who enriched themselves out of the purchase of Abbey lands at Sawley and out of forfeited estates of the Hamertons. A claim made by Sir Arthur Darcy to use part of Champion Common is mentioned under Champion.

Witnesses in the above case were : Alan Bradley of Chipping, gent., aged 40 ; John Heslett of Slaidburne, aged 60 ; Thomas Parker of Greystoneley, aged 40.[1]

A Forest Dispute in 1554.

In this dispute the aforementioned Ralph Greenacres, together with Richard Assheton, John Walmesley, and Anthony Coulthurst, were brought before the Duchy Court by John Tempest and Thomas Parker, gentlemen. These two gentlemen complain that they leased from the Queen (Mary) on 29th November, 1553, the herbage and pasturage of 6 closes called Lelonde, Whitewell Green, Foster Close, Cleesholme, Long Knot, and Whitmore, containing 80 acres at the yearly rent of £6.13s.4d. These lands were forcibly retained by the defendants in the case.

The closes mentioned are New Laund at Whitewell, and various lands extending towards Farrick, above which are the Knot and Whitmore. Cleeholme or Clayholme is in the same direction.

[1] Smith, p. 182.

On August 22 1554 evidence was taken at Lancaster, before Sir Edward Saunders and William Dallyson.

Christopher Parker, aged about 39, said that the closes belonged to the Queen, and that Richard Assheton had depastured the closes for 5 or 6 years contrary to established custom. Before this time the 6 closes had been used as deer pasture, except that in summer the Master Forester kept 2 geldings in the Lawnd, and the Deputy Foresters used part of the closes called Green Lawnd, Foster Close, and Cliveholme.

The red and fallow deer number only about 300, although there is pasture for 1000 more.

Sir Thomas Langton, says that in the times of the late Lord Monteagle (1494-1523) there were 2000 deer in the Forest.

Much of the evidence in this dispute is tedious and unimportant. However, the document is a useful indication of some of the principal inhabitants of Bolland at this time, especially as their ages are given :

Christopher Parker, 39
John Dobson, 55
Robert Sherborn, gent. 63
Christopher Mawdsley 70
Bryan Parker, 80
John Waller, 60
Anthony Langton, gent., 60
Thomas Bound, 60
Robert Bound, 60
William Banyster, gent., 52
Christopher Swinglehurst, 57
Rowland Parker, 50
Alexander Parker, 90
Robert Bound, 70
John Robinson, 71
Nicholas Turner, 53
Robert Turner, 48
Thomas Parker of Harden, 54
James Coltleys, 72
Peter Hall, 70
Henry Colthurst, 70
Henry Goodday, 66
Reginald Parker, 52
James Bleysdall, 56
Henry Wyddelldale of Slaidburn (Whitendale), 50
Christopher Browne or Whitteldale, 40
Henry Bleysdall, 70
George Wrangell, 60

Alexander Parker could remember Sir James Harrington as Master Forester, appointed 1485.

Two years later another Commission made a survey of the deer and reported that there were 134 red deer and 146 fallow. Upon Burnslack with Giles Harrison and Robert Marton as keepers there were 52 red deer. Upon Whynfell with Thomas Proctor as keeper there were 30 red deer. Upon Tottridge there were three keepers—Reginald Parker had 28 red and 40 fallow ; Robert Swinlehurst had 13 red and 78 fallow ; and Alan Bradley had 2 red and 13 fallow. Within "the drifts and outsides of the forest" there were 7 red and 5 fallow. Within Radom Park there were 2 red and 10 fallow.

The same Commission surveyed the trees and timber. They report : Timber trees being saplings...710. Sapling stubs...524. Ashes...93. Saplings east and south of the Lees within the office of Alan Bradley...500, but of these 200 were very small.

There is an unusual item about some of the ash-trees. Some are very old and hollow "on account of frequent cropping for the deer in times past."

Much is only fit for firewood, and the rest only fit for gate-stoops and for gates and sills in poor men's houses. All the rest of the Bolland woods are "old hollins, old heythornes, old hassilles, old crabtrees and oller-wood." The ollers or alders grow in great abundance in "carres and marysshes" and do damage to the grazing. Some of these old trees, old hollies, crab-apples, and the rest have survived in at least one of the larger fields at Stakes.

No mention is made of the elm, which today is one of the most numerous trees by the Hodder.

More so than in many villages, this pub, the **Hark to Bounty**, was a centre of community life. Evidence of this is that it incorporated a court room where justice was dispensed. The room was reached by the stone steps. The outer edge of the steps, outside the iron railing, were used as mounting steps to enable folk to get on their horses.

CHAPTER XV.

GENTLEMEN POACHERS.

From the end of the Middle Ages the gradual encroachment of farms on the Forest lands must have diminished the number of the deer, but perhaps the chief cause for the steady decline in their numbers was the excessive slaughter by poachers. In 1524 Sir Richard Tempest, "the Master Foster" or Forester, accused Sir Richard Houghton of having slaughtered 21 deer within a year and a half.

One of the illicit hunting expeditions of Sir Richard Houghton is described by himself in answer to various charges :

Upon St. Wilfrid's day last, about the going down of the sun, he went to a chace of his own adjoining the forest of Bolland, called Chipping Common, intending to have a course and espied two hinds and set for them with his greyhounds. The hinds fled followed by the dogs to a place called Cold Byrkes a mile within the Forest, where the hounds were taken up, having killed no deer. Returning homewards in a high way leading through the forest close to a place called Tunstall Hyng, three persons met him and without any words spekyng shot him and his servants. The latter in order to avoid the arrows, were obliged to loose the dogs and to return the shots. Thereupon the attacking party beat a retreat and finding Sir Richard's greyhounds at large in a bankside, killing a grey, took them and presented them to Nicholas Tempest the Deputy Forester of Bolland.

This Nicholas Tempest may have been the member of the Tempest family who was executed at Tyburn for his part in the Pilgrimage of Grace.

Some years later, namely in 1532, the Master Forester, Sir Thomas Clifford, laid a complaint against Robert Singleton, gentleman, no doubt of Daub Hall for having killed a buck in Laygryme park. The Forester desired that the Chancellor of the Duchy should question him as to the number of times he had hunted by day and by night, with what company and how many deer were killed. Two members of his family admitted in evidence that their kinsman had several times killed as many as 12 deer in a night's hunting.

Another illicit hunt organised by Thomas Houghton, son and heir of Sir Richard Houghton, was reported to have taken place on February 14th, 1558. Thomas Houghton was accompanied by a numerous gathering which included Richard Houghton, gentleman, Robert Winder, Richard Cottam, Henry Wilkinson of Grymesarghe, Thomas Tipping, George Beesley of Gosenarghe, William Craven, Smith, Richard Thorneley of Chepin, Henry Thornely, Robert Thornely, James Helme of the Black Moss, Thomas Rodes of Elmerege, William Rhodes, John Threlfall, John Richmond, John Halton, Robert Clarke, Edmund Bounde, Thomas Startivant, gentleman, Edward Cottam of Ribchester, and others. They went into a close called Scolehirst Hey, "used as a drift by the officers of the Forest". They took captive John Dobson, one of the keepers, and then proceeded to hunt and kill two great stags.

One of the accused, Richard Thorneley, made a reply that is worth quoting. He said that on the day in question he had gone to hear Mass at the Church in Chipping. He described himself as a charterer to Sir Richard Houghton and he heard at church that certain deer were in Scolehirst Hey, which was the freehold of his master. Accordingly, he went along with Thomas Houghton to see the deer chased.[1]

Another example of poaching, this time with cross-bows and hand-guns, as they were called, occurs in 1572 when Sir Richard Sherburne lays a complaint against Roger and Anthony Knolles of Bradford near Clitheroe. They were accused of disregarding the law passed in the 30th year of the reign of Henry VIII against the use of the crossbow. These men had killed a deer in the West Clough and had hit another in a certain place called Knoll pasture.

Nicholas Assheton has several references to hunting in Bolland in his Journal for 1617. We read : "1617, Sept. 6. All but Mr. Chancellor into Bolland. At Stable Oak. A stag killed at Harden and another a little above, which made excellent sport . . . Sept. 17 to Batterise : to Burnside and Whitendale, overrun with good deare. A knubb (two-year old stag) was killed and a calf . . . Nov. 15. On hill above Walloper Well shott two young hinds; presently comes the keeper and broke the other deere, had the skin and a shoulder and 5s. and said hee would take noe notice."

In view of the continual poaching of the deer by local gentlemen and others, it is not surprising that in a survey dated October 12, 1652 we find that of red deer, stags, hinds and calves there were only 20, and of fallow deer only 40.

The centuries show the gradual decrease in the number of the deer, although Whitaker records that in 1805 a fine herd of wild deer were destroyed, "the last vestige of feudal superiority" in the ancient Forest.[2]

[1] If we may leave deer-hunting for a moment, it may be of interest to some if certain information is given at this point about the Thomas Houghton mentioned above. In view of his devotion to the old religion it is likely that he would have attended the Mass at Chipping. He succeeded to the estate in this same year 1558 and proceeded to build the present Hoghton Tower. Yet he sacrificed his estate and rank in 1569 when he sailed secretly down the Ribble heading for the Low Countries, where he was to live in exile for eleven years because he would not accept Queen Elizabeth's changes of religion. He never returned to the land he loved but died in exile and was buried at St. Gervais in Liege, Belgium. He had been accompanied abroad by his son Thomas, who eventually came back to England as a priest but was cast into Salford gaol, where he probably died after two years' confinement.

[2] The documents upon which the facts in this chapter are based were first printed in Smith's *Hist. of Chipping*, pp. 187-190.

CHAPTER XVI.

THE LEAGRIM AND CASTLESTEAD SURVEY.

In the 34th year of Elizabeth I a Royal Commission was set up to enquire into the Bolland Forest boundary near Bleasdale, Chipping and Leagrim. The members of the Commission were Sir Richard Sherburne, Rauffe Ashton, Thomas Preston, Thomas Talbot, esquires, Richard Greenacres, and John Dewhurst gent. Evidence was taken at Leagrim itself, the name being written Laithegryme.

The chief questions asked local farmers and shepherds were concerning the setting out of new boundaries, by stakes, stones, and hills made as boundary marks. The reference to the hills made as boundaries is worth noting, as it indicates that some of the old mounds and piles of stones belong to the time of Elizabeth rather than to the Middle Ages. One question is worth quoting in full as it gives details of the boundary between Bolland, Bleasdale and Chipping.

Beginning at the Queen Majesty's forest of Bleesedall at a certain clough which doth divide Chippen and Bleesedall called Meareclough, and so following the bound between Chippen and Bowland to Wynyate, and so to Whetstoneclough head of Bleesedall, that divides Bolland Bleesedall and Chippen, and from thence to Grinlawe cloughe head to the height of the Saddle, and so to the quirke of the Saddle, and so from thence to the upper end of Threaplee, and so following the outside of Threaplee to the Windiehills hey, and so following the outside of Windiehills hey to a place called Braydley, and so to Pecocke brook, and so down as Pecocke brook runs to Chippen brook and so down the middle stream of Chippen brook unto Lowde.

Peacock Hey farm today indicates that Pecocke brook is now called Dobson's brook. It is curious that the same paragraph spells Bolland in two different ways, as indicated in the text.

The witnesses who gave evidence were William Swynlehurste of Harden, Richard Parker of Lickhurst, William Dobson of Wardsley, John Waller of Leagrim, Henry Bleesedall of Inckline-green, Raynold Parker of Graystonlee, Thomas Halton of Halton Heyes in Lancashire, Robert Gregson of Leagrim, Arthur Parker the elder of Lickhurst, William Coore of Coorehowse in Chippen, John Parker of Harden, John Harryson of Harden, and John Swinlehurste of Farrockhowse.

The question of Castlestead was discussed with some of the witnesses because one of the matters in dispute was whether a place called Castlesteede had been occupied as part of Burnslack. William Swynlehurste of Harden asserted that one Richard Parker of Lickhurst, grandfather of the present occupier, placed his cattle in the Castlesteede on the west side of Burnslack brook. Richard Parker testified in the same way, saying that his grandfather Richard and his father Ellis held half of the Burnslack and a Bryan Parker held the other half. Their land went to the height of the Saddle, as heaven water deals, then to the quirk of the Saddle, then to Threepelee, and they also depastured on a place called Castlesteede.

The evidence of John Waller of Leagrim Park has a few personal touches. His father had no right of common in the waste at Chippen and used to send his sheep for pasture to Bryan Parker, who held half of Burnslack. The sheep were mostly kept at a place called Castlesteede and upon a bank at the east side of the quirk of the Saddle. He says that he himself has driven his grandmother's sheep by friendship of the tenant of Burnslack to depasture in the Castlesteede and the rest of the bank under the Saddle.

Raynold Parker of Graystonelee testifies about the Forest boundaries and adds that he has heard John Swinlehurst say that his father Robert Swinlehurst, being deputy under Sir Richard Sherburne, did kill a deer between the height of the Saddle and Burnslack brook and took the same away without interruption from any person.

Arthur Parker of Lickhurst said that Bryan Parker used to get turf for his dwelling-house in Burnslack from a moss between Threepelee and the Saddle, and on the west of Burnslack brook. This dwelling-house would probably be on the site where Ward's End was later built, and shows that the two farming sites on the Burnslack are quite old. Ward's End is no longer inhabited.

One witness, Thomas Halton, recalls the picture of a Bolland scene that has vanished for ever, when he describes how he used to drive the deer from out of Bleasdale and over the Saddle. From that we gather that some of the deer wandered at large over Bolland.

Note on Castlestead.

How many Lancashire people know that there is a place in Lancashire called Castlestead ? It is not on any map, and it is not in any guide book. On the hills that look towards Lancaster and Morecambe Bay there is a place called Abbeystead, the site where the monks first settled before they went to Furness Abbey. Castlestead is on the eastern side of the same hills and dominates the valley of the Ribble. This chapter may help to put Castlestead on the map and to make it known as it deserves to be known. At present it has been known to only about a dozen persons at most.

Who know Castlestead ?

Some of the farmers who have tended sheep on the Bleasdale fells above Chipping have kept alive the old name of Castlestead. There are not many in the district today who could tell you where to find it.

The present writer, studying Bolland Forest history with a friend, came across the old name in a survey dating back to Queen Elizabeth I. This survey is now preserved in the Public Record Office in London. It is curious that the only known statement about the old name is preserved in London.

What is Castlestead ?

Is Castlestead just an unusual name that has almost been lost? There is evidence to show that it is more than a mere name.

First of all, what does the name mean ? It means the site of a castle or fort. The first thought of an Englishman when he hears the word castle is of the stately stone strongholds of the Normans —Windsor, the great monuments of Conway and Caernarvon, and our own Lancaster and Clitheroe. Yet castle can mean an ancient earthwork, as witness the well-known fortress of the ancient Britons known as Maiden Castle.

If you visit the Castlestead of Ribblesdale you will realise long before you reach it that it could not be a stone castle but an ancient earthwork fortress.

Where is Castlestead ?

The student of the old document from Queen Elizabeth I's reign now in the Public Record Office can find that a place called Castlestead existed in the fells above Chipping but he would have a hard task to find the exact place, if he had only the old records to guide him. Fortunately there are still in the district a handful of people who can point out the place that the deed calls "Castle steede". It was the good fortune of the present writer to find, more by good luck than management, one of the very few living who know where Castlestead is to be found.

The Castlestead of today.

It was only when a young sheep-farmer had pointed out to our exploration party the site of Castlestead on a distant hill that we realised the full meaning and interest of such a name in the remote and inaccessible country where it lay. Even today the only easy approach to Castlestead would be by helicopter. The train stops fifteen miles away ; the bus stops five or six miles away; and a car can only reach within at least two miles of rough going, and the last half mile is steep climbing. The last half mile would daunt any except the very young or the most determined, as it is one of the steepest gradients in these hills.

The man-made line.

The explorer of these remote hills is not a man that the sheep-farmer meets very often. Even in these days when ramblers get into the most unexpected places, the ancient site of Castlestead keeps its aloofness—it is so far away from the beaten tracks, and it is so far away from the unbeaten tracks. If it was chosen as a last outpost by the ancient Britons, they chose well, because even in this age of easy communications it has rarely been visited by the foot of man. A man climbing up the extraordinarily steep gradient out of the remote valley of the Burnslack brook might never notice signs of the works of man. Yet if you are looking for Castlestead you see at once a man-made line.

Castlestead is rightly called a "castle".

Anybody who has the courage and the endurance to set out on foot and explore the hills that surround the steep valley of the Burnslack brook, which finds its way eventually into the Hodder, will see the line of Castlestead. It is an artificial rim high up on the steep face of the hill. It is just like several acknowledged earth-work defences of the early Britons in different parts of England's hill country.

Behind its shelter a crowd of men, women, and children, together with a number of domestic animals could find a temporary protection. Here was an unfailing spring of fresh water. Here was an amount of sparse fodder for beasts. Here from the military point of view was a supreme place of vantage, for from here the valleys of the Hodder and the Ribble could be surveyed for miles, and any newcomer into these valleys would be a long time before he found his way into the remote fastness of the hills.

Even the curling smoke of a fire on the hill fort would in most weathers pass for a low cloud or a mountain mist.

Only digging can give definite proof.

What is the evidence that we can forward to suggest that Castlestead might be a British fort ?

1. The name is ancient and therefore suggests something unusual to earn such an unusual name.

2. Castle on a hill site often means an ancient earthwork. In the south of England such works are more common than in the north.

3. There seems to be a man-made ridge high above the valley of Burnslack where Castlestead lies according to old tradition.

4. This ridge is a superb natural fortress in so far as it dominates the surrounding country for miles and is at the head of a remote valley, even today far removed from the ordinary ways and haunts of men.

5. Round the corner from Castlestead—that is only a few miles round a bend in the hills—is the ancient British site generally called the Bleasdale Circle. It is an ancient British burial ground and its presence not far from the hill site of Castlestead is a proof that the primitive people of Britain were no strangers to these hills.

Exploration by the spade might provide some proof more tangible that Castlestead was a fortified place of ancient Britain.

(Based on Public Record Office—Duchy of Lancaster Special Commissions No. 497.)

Brownsholme Hall, seat from ancient times of the Parker family, whose history is inextricably intertwined with that of the Forest of Bolland and the Hodder Valley. The hall was built by the family in 1507.

CHAPTER XVII.

LEAGRIM HALL AND CHIPPING LAWND.

The story of Leagrim goes back to the Middle Ages, and it first became important when it became a Lodge or a kind of shooting box for the Forester of Little Bolland, or that part of the Forest that was included in Lancashire after the Norman Conquest. The oldest forms of the name always begin with *Laithe,* which stands for a barn. Perhaps the Hall had such humble beginnings.

From 1410 onwards the de Hoghton family were very often the official Keepers of Leagrim, although after the Wars of the Roses Lord Monteagle brought the Stanley interest into the region. The story of Leagrim from that time forward is one of decline as a forest for deer, and at the same time a story of the increase of farming because of the clearing away of old forest trees. In 1555 at the beginning of the reign of Mary Tudor, Leagrim was declared to be no longer a royal park. The royal decree states that there are scarcely any wild cattle or deer left, and that trees and underwood have been laid waste to keep up the *Pale,* or deer-fence. Sir Richard Shireburne was granted the tenancy of the lands with permission to fell trees and make enclosures.[1]

In 1562 Queen Elizabeth bestowed Leagrim upon her favourite Dudley, Earl of Leicester, who promptly sold it to the lessee, Sir Richard Shireburne of Stonyhurst. This purchase by the Shireburnes meant that in the coming centuries Leagrim would become a centre of Catholic Recusants. It passed from the Shireburnes to the Weld family.

The old local name for the deer park at Leagrim is Chipping Lawnd, a name that is now attached to the farm beyond the Hall. A lawnd in old English generally described an enclosure for deer.

Weld in his history of Leagrim[2] pointed out that even today, centuries after the deer-park had ceased to be, there were traces of the old ditch and palisade which had been built with much cost and labour in the Middle Ages. According to Weld there was a ditch four feet deep and eight feet wide, planted with three rows of thorns, and on the outside of the thorns there was a high fence of oak palings. Even the most agile of the deer would be prevented by the ditch filled with thorns from approaching the outer palisade.

In view of the fact that the history of Leagrim has been written, the most useful purpose to be served by the present survey

[1] Smith in his *History of Chipping,* 193-194, prints part of the decree.
[2] Chetham Soc.

may be to complete past records by an account of the old park ditch and boundary as it was traced recently nearly 400 years after the deer-fence had ceased to be cared for. It is indeed remarkable that in spite of centuries of neglect and in spite of the increased cultivation of land, how much of the old ditch can be traced today. To those who love to trace the work and ways of past generations there can be as much thrill and excitement in tracing the old foss and *vallum* or ditch and earthwork of Chipping Lawnd as for those who trace Offa's Dike or the line of the Roman Wall between Tyne and Solway.

A farm like the Pale near Chipping informs the student of the past that by its name alone it must have stood either inside or outside the old deer-park fence, as this old barrier was often called the Pale. If we stop to reason about this, we should say that the farm must have been outside the Pale, otherwise the deer would have destroyed the farmer's crops. In fact, if we examine the map, we find that even today the Pale farm is outside the Leagrim boundary, but is classed with it as part of Little Bolland. On the large scale ordnance survey the Leagrim boundary by the Pale marks the line of the old deer-fence, whereas the Little Bolland boundary follows the line of the Loud, and along part of Chipping Brook, making a detour to include Red Bank before becoming identical with the Leagrim boundary as it leaves the Pale.

A good distance of the old ditch can be traced from the Pale to the fields above Loud Mytham. Opposite Green Lands farm, which may have been Green Lawnd, there is an unusual lay-out of the land by the stepping stones of Bailey Hippings. Incidentally, the word Hippings for stepping-stones seems to have quite gone out of use.

The large-scale map can be used for tracing the old ditch from above Loud Mytham to Leagram Mill, which it leaves on the west. From this point up to Park Gate, for well over a mile, the line of the ditch can be traced with ease and in some places the old thorns are still standing on the slope below where the fence ran. The stretch from the Pale to the fields above Loud Mytham and this stretch above Leagrim brook are easily the best preserved sections of the time-worn boundary.

An old Leagrim map marks Pymlines on the outside of the fence by Leagrim brook, and Park Close Style in Pymlines, which is very probably the Park Style of today. Pymlines may represent the line of the Pins or fence-poles. The same map marks Aklaye above Wardsley, the Ack or Oak being a reminder of the giants of the forest that are now no more, but Weld's history reminds us that some of the great black stumps of the primeval oaks have been unearthed in Chipping Moss and many no doubt still lie there.

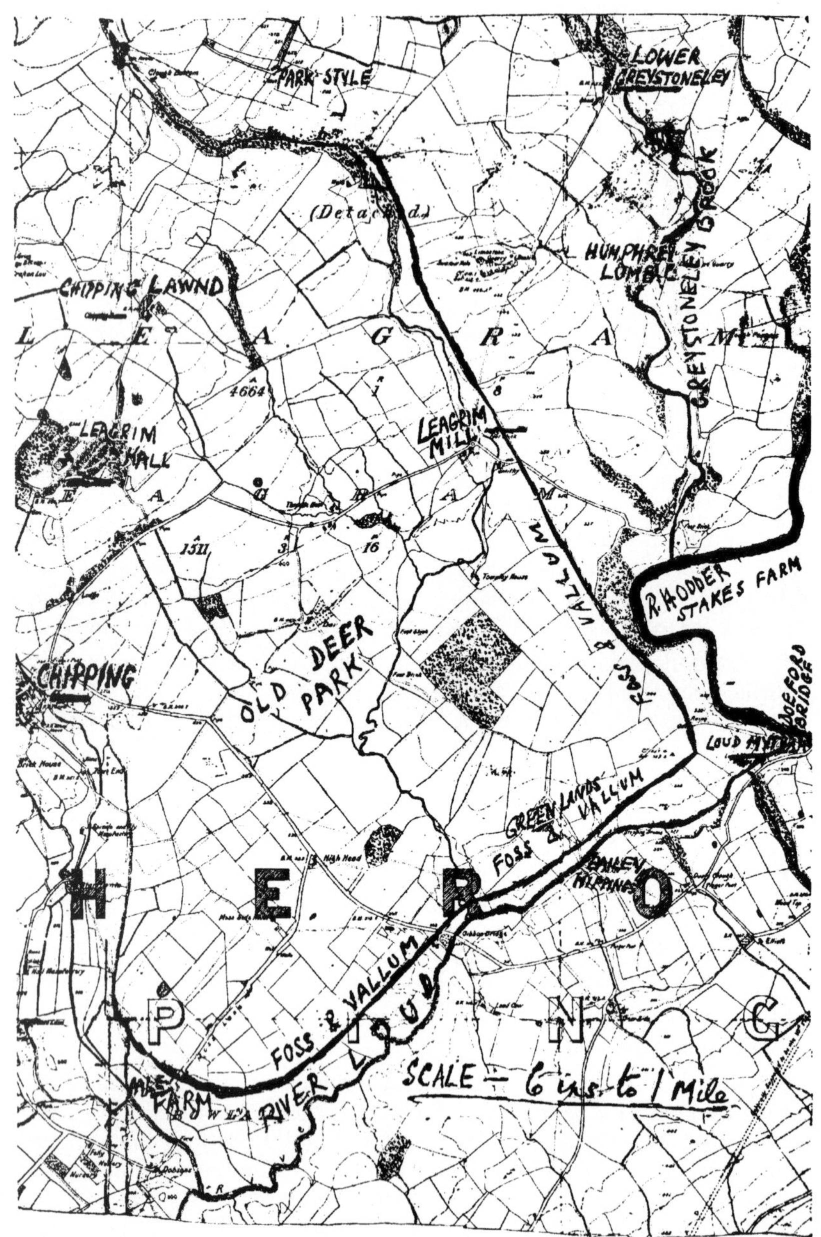

LEAGRIM DEER PARK—FOSS & VALLUM.

From Park Gate, which was once Walker Yatt, it is not always easy to determine the line of the deer-park, because to the north and west of the Lodge the line of the estate does not seem to have been the same as the line of the deer-fence. It may have come from Park Gate in the direction of Chipping Lawn. On the evidence at present available it has not been possible to determine satisfactorily the line of the fence and ditch on the northern and western side in the neighbourhood of the Lodge or Hall. It is possible that the fence ran from Chipping Lawn below the Lodge towards Chipping brook and Chipping village, where Green Lane reminds us of an older name Park Green. In this way the home farm of the Lodge would have been kept clear of the invasions and ravages of the wandering herds of deer.

A weekly visitor to many Bolland farms was Mr Clayton, a Settle-based grocer whose staff, horse and cart are seen here at their best, probably just after an agricultural show.

CHAPTER XVIII.

THE FOREST IN 1596.

A document of unusual interest gives us a good picture of the state of Bolland Forest in Queen Elizabeth's day. This document is the report drawn up "at the Whytewell" on September 27th, 1596, by the Queen's Commissioners, who had been sent there to enquire into the state of the Forest after the death of the Master Forester, Sir Richard Sherburne. The Commissioners were Rauffe Assheton, High Sheriff of Lancashire, Richard Houghton, Thomas Talbot, and James Anderton. It may be remarked in passing that this Richard Houghton, who was then twenty-six years of age, was destined to be the first baronet of the famous family of Houghton Tower.

The Commissioners had been sent a long list of questions about which evidence was to be taken on oath. These questions are chiefly about the illegal felling of trees or the illegal killing of the Queen's deer. Quite apart from the information to be found about timber and the game preserves, the Commission records so many names of persons and of the places where they dwell that it provides a unique piece of evidence about the old families settled in the Forest area.[1]

The first witness examined was Sir Richard Sherburne's deputy keeper William Swinglehurst of Harden, of the age of 44 — "sworn and examined, to the first interrogatory says he has known the Forest for about twenty years."

To the second question he says that "he has heard of divers timber trees and others cut down within the last five years."

He then names several men for felling trees :

James Tomlinson of Bashall—1 tree
William Blesdall of Thinklingreen—one stubb tree for the repair of his fyerhouse.
Stephen Harrison of Batteres—five stub trees or powls
William Marton of Batteres—2 or 3 stub trees
Robert Parkinson—2 stub trees
Robert Bleasdell younger of the Lees—12 stub trees or powls
Stephen Knowles—1 powl
Adam Holgate—2 stub trees

The record adds that the witness for "further certainty refereth himself to his books."

To the third question the witness "deposeth and saith that he having his houses in decay and for want of timber apt for building, did make exchange with Henry Aulston of Chippin and Robert

[1] Public Record Office—Duchy of Lancaster Special Commissions No. 520.

Parker of the same of some auld timber trees for some young timber . . . "

To the fourth question "he deposeth and saith that three years ago there was a view and certificate made of Her Majesty's game of deer within the forest of Bowlland and Raddum park to the Chancellor of the Duchy and of one thousand and above of red and fallow deer, viz. the one half of red and the other half of fallow or thereabout ; and there remaineth but now in the forest and park of red and fallow deer to the number of eight hundred or thereabout and that there died in the winter last past thirteen score or thereabout."

To the fifth question he replies "that there hath been divers of her Majesty's game of deer as well red as fallow have been killed or destroyed without warrant in the forest and park within five years last past, as may appear by a certain information exhibited in the Duchy in Hillary term last year or thereabout."

The sixth question was as to whether the keepers or other officers "had served any process against any malefactors or trespassers against the Queen's deer." To this Swinglehurst replied "that the keepers and other officers have proceeded against divers offenders within the forest of Bowlland and elsewhere, as may appear by the said information in the Duchy . . . except Olliver Cottam and Richard Parkinson which could not be met withal, and to this deponent's knowledge none of the offenders have appeared except John Whyppe, and that one Robert Dewhurst and Robert Parkinson of the Woodhouse did contribute to the charge of the process (legal action) and entered bond or promised bond for their good behaviour by direction from Sir Richard Sherburne, and further that John Bound and divers others the inhabitants of Wyersdale near unto the confines of both the forests of Boulland and Wyersdale did kill a hind about March last, and upon request of Mr. Tunstall and Mr. Crage and others, the said Sir Richard was contented to spare their appearance, some of them being contributors for the process, and upon proffer of security for their good behaviour."

The next four questions mention various persons by name on the charge of poaching and more information is asked about them. Question 7 : "Whether do you know that George Harrison of Batteraxe, Thomas Parkinson of Brennand, Christopher Parker of Lyckehurst, Robert Bee of Batteraxe, James Fletcher of Chippin, and Thomas Swinglehurst of Burowholme (Burholme), or any of them have destroyed any of Her Majesty's game or made any spoil of Her Majesty's woods within the said Forest."

Question 8 : "Whether do you know Alexander Turner, Robert Sherburne, and John Whippe, or any of them, and whether did not the said Turner in June 1594 kill a young stag at Batteraxe with a dog which did belong to William Swinglehurst, and whether have not the said Sherburne and Whippe hunted divers times in the said forest."

Question 9: "Whether do you know that John Whitaker, Christopher Simonson, Nicholas Battersbie, Richard Battersbie, Robert Parkinson, John Whyppe, Olliver Cottam, Richard Parkinson, Richard Sowthen, Christopher Battersbie, Ambros Mitton, James Oddie, Thomas Walmisley, Edward Collinson, Hughe Kydd, John Lawe and Robert Dewhurst, or any of them to have hunted or killed any game or deer."

Question 10: "Whether did not Ellis Broughton of Bashall Eves, James Bauker and Robert Walmsley, or any of them hunt in the night time within the said forest about St. Andrew's day last past."

The records do not mention any reply to question 7, but state that to the 8th, 9th and 10th, the witness gives evidence as in the reply to question 6. From which it would seem that the witness was rather unwilling to make any serious charge. The general impression of the whole proceedings is that most of charges are somewhat glossed over. This would be following the precedent set by Sir Richard Sherburne when Master Forester. According to the evidence just mentioned, he seems to have been willing to treat offenders with great leniency—a thing which often happened when the old country squires administered a rough and ready justice in their countryside and for "their own people".

The eleventh question brings further charges: "Whether do you know that on the 13th day of July last past, being Sunday, John Talbott, John Haulton, and Thomas Walmsley or any of them did hunt in Raddum Park at the Queen's game with dogs and guns and such like, and did not they or some of them kill a deer in Raddum Park . . . " The witness says "that he hath heard by Robert Rawthemell and James Parker, keeper of the Lees and others, the said parties . . . named did kill a deer in Raddum Park or in the Forest."

After this there appears some confusion in the records. The official list of questions passes from number 11 to number 13, although the evidence of the witness provides an answer to a question 12. "To the 12th interrogatory he deposeth and saith as he has heard by report of Richard Houlden, gentleman, that the said Richard Houlden of Chageley did kill a stag in Chageley in August last within his feudal demesne in Chageley, which he (this witness) taketh to be not part of the forest of Bolland."

The official list of questions has an interesting number 13, but the evidence of the witness contains no reference to it whatsoever.

Even without an answer Question 13 in the official list is one full of interest. Question 13 : "Whether do you know or have heard that Thomas Parkinson of Brennand had one hind calf found hid in fleeces of wool in his chamber ; whether was not in July last a stag's head new cut off found near to Stotte Close, and one hind in Wardsley, and who did kill the same, as you have heard, and as you think in your conscience."

From Brennand to Wardsley via Stot Close (opposite Burholme) is a long stretch of miles and gives some indication of the range then enjoyed by the deer.

The records now put down an answer to question 14 as though it were an answer to number 13. Either the clerks of the Commission were very careless or there was some juggling with the list of questions and answers.

Question 14 is about Lagram. "He deposeth and saith the said ground called Lagram Park late the inheritance of Sir Richard Sherburne knight deceased, and that the said Park is fenced with hedge and ditch for the most part thereof, and some payle staykes, and that the deer of the forest have recourse into the said park and that likewise the deer of the park have small recourse into the said forest of Bowland."

The reference to "payle staykes" or fence poles is of special interest as both words survive as farm names. Pale Farm is near Chipping and Stakes Farm is by the Hodder just across from Little Bolland.

Question 15 is also about Lagram. "He saith that he hath known divers deer stricken or killed in the said park of Lagram since the death of Sir Richard Sherburne knight viz.: 5 stags and 3 or 4 bucks[1] or thereabouts, and how one of the said 5 stags one whereof was called Wegehorn (Wedgehorn?) was stricken in the park and fled into the forest and there was found and killed by the Master Forester, and given to Richard Sherburn Esquire . . . "

The next witness was Renolde Parker one of the woodwards of the Forest. He says "that all the timber felled without warrant before April last remain in the records of the Swaynmote Court, yet since the Court there has been felled without warrant one ash by himself to repair his house and thereof did make Sir Richard Sherburn knight then officer acquainted, also by William Bleasdall one pale by the like licence of Sir Richard as afforesaid."

"Robert Dobson his son in law hathe felled and carried out of the Forest 2 stub trees."

This witness gave unfavourable evidence about the state of Lagram Park. In fact we know that Lagram had ceased to be a

[1] Stags are taken to be red deer and bucks the fallow deer.

deer park some forty years before, and so it is not surprising to hear that its fences were poor.

"He saith that he knows the said ground called Lagram Park and that there is no fence made about the said park, but that the deer of the Forest and the deer of the said park hath and may have free course and intercourse betwixt the said ground at their pleasures."

"He saith that he certainly knoweth not how many deer have been stricken and killed in the said park since the death of Sir Richard Sherburn, but to his remembrance there was 3 or 4 bucks and 2 or 3 stags or thereabouts, whereof one of the stags as he hath credibly heard was stricken in the said park of Lagram by William Swinglehurst and after pursued by the said Swinglehurst and Mr. Hugh Sherburn and divers others into the said forest of Bolland and there killed in Wardesley, being parcel of the forest, and taken away by them out of the forest, and further that one other old known deer called Wegghorn was stricken by William Swinglehurst in the park afforesaid, and fled into the said forest and afterwards was killed by the Master Forester."

Thomas Haulton, age 36, was the next witness. He confirms the statement of Renold Parker about the bad state of the Lagram fences and states that "there have been six stags and five bucks stricken or killed in the said park of Laythgram."

Arthur Parker, aged 60, followed. He gives evidence about tree felling. "There have been divers trees felled in the forest within the five years last past about the Whytewell in Bowland by four of the Queen's tenants viz. Robert Parker—1 tree, Anthony Parker—2 trees, William Swinglehurst—1 tree, but to what value this deponent cannot certainly depose, and that he himself by delindie (licence) of the Woodwards 1 tree in the tenement of James Roodes, and within his own tenement upon the Lees—3 stub trees and 1 ash for sparres to the firehouse, and 2 stub trees within his own tenement at the Lyckehurst, and that Robert Parker his son did fell 1 stub tree upon the Lees, by whose delindie he cannot depose."

As regards the killing of deer, he admits "that his wife and Peter his son did take and kill one Sower (   ) and for the same was presented at the next court after the same committed, and thereof upon hearing of the same before Sir Richard Sherburn knight, then officer, was thereupon before him discharged."

The next witness called was Reynold Sawer, aged 33. (We know from other sources that the Sawers were at Burholme about this time, and their name is kept alive by a "Sawer Barn" nearby. It is not surprising, then, that Reynold Sawer should speak about Burholme.) "He saith that one Thomas Swinglehurst of Burrowholme, one of Her Majesty's tenants in the said forest have taken

. . . 2 pair of croockes with some other timber and hath builded the same upon the upper inheritance of the said Swinglehurst and out of the forest . . . "

George Harrison of Batterax was examined next. He admits that one of his servants killed a deer. "One Alexander Turner, servant to this witness being sent by his master to gather timber, a greyhound which this witness did keep did follow the said Turner and by chance did kill a twinter deer, viz. a knubbe (a knubbe or knobber is a two year old stag) and was called for the same before William Swinglehurst, the deputy steward, but what order was taken in the same the witness cannot depose."

The last statement rather shows that the deputy steward was not too severe, like his late master, Sir Richard Sherburn.

Thomas Swinglehurst of Burrowholme (Burholme) followed as a witness. He admits "that this last year he has cut down only by delindie (exemption) of the rest of the Woodwards without other warrant 3 stub trees in the park of Raddum, and in the rest of the said five years he has cut down, but to what number or value he cannot depose, and further that Thomas Parkinson hath cut down by delindie of the four men (the Woodwards) one hollow stub tree and one poule, George Harrison of Batterax 2 poules . . . . He (this witness) has had the charge and custody of the park of Radham in the time of the weakness of Sir Richard Sherburn, late Master Keeper there . . . One Henry Ballarde did confess that he bought of one James Cooke one doe skin and a fawn skin which this witness supposes were of stolen deer."

Another session was held on the first day of October at which a jury of 13 men presented certain charges. The 13 were Olliver Marton, Thomas Turner of Lees, James Rodes, William Bleasdall, Robert Parker of Sykes, James Parker of Thorneholme, John Parker of Harden, James Parker of Lees, Robert Rauthmell, Thomas Parker of Graystonelee, William Marton of Batteres, Arthur Parker the elder of Lykehurst, Robert Wytendall.

The following are the charges :

- Ollyver Marton doth present himself for felling 6 sapling powlles within his own ground for the repair of his old barn, worth every powlle 6d.

- We present Peter Lamb for felling 3 dotered (docked?) ellers within Radham Parke, each eller worth 4d.

- we present Reynold Parker for felling 1 ash stub given him by Sir Richard Sherburn for the repair of his fyerhowse—worth 12d.

- William Bleasdall doth present himself for felling 1 sapling powle worth 16d.

- We present William Swinglehurst of Harden for felling 1 ash powle . . . worth 6d.

- We present Thomas Typpinge of the Farr for felling 1 hollow oak stub and carrying the same out of the forest . . . worth 6d.

- Arthur Parker the elder doth present himself for felling of 2 sapling stubs for the repair of his fyerhowse—worth 8d.

- Robert Rauthmell doth present himself for felling 2 sapling powles for the repair of one barn . . . worth 4d.

As most of the charges are alike from this point onwards the document is only printed in brief.

- Thomas Houghton of Chadgley for felling.

- Robert Bleasdall younger for felling.

- Edward Parker, servant to James Rudds of the Stakes, killing some does or other fallow deer.

- One knobbe being killed by a dog at the house of George Harrison of Batteres, that followed his servants to the fell, viz. Alexander Turner and John Harrison.

- One knobbe being killed in burn of fire, but we know not by whom.

- James Tomlinson of Bashall Eves for felling.

- Adam Houlgate for felling.

- William Marton of Batteres for felling.

- Peter Lamb for felling.

- Reynolde Parker was given to understand by one of the tenants at Lykehurst that he had followed the corn-field hedge about and had found in one of his nebors part of the hedge one rope set to destroy Her Majesty's game and did watch the same and by fortune all the tenants followed the hedge about and did find the gap and stopped the hole and left the rope behind them.

- Mr. Robert Tempest for his dog ranging forth from his man and killing one fawn.

- Ellis Broughton of Bashall Eves, James Bawker, Thomas Middleton with others for hunting upon Andrew's day at night last, whose names we could never know before this time.

- Mr. John Talbot, John Hewlton, Thomas Walmsley of Bashall Eves, for hunting upon the 14th day of July last, being Sunday, at night and killing one doe within Radhame Park and carrying the same away to Nicholas Houlden his house of Bashall Eves.

- Mr. Richard Houlden of Chadgley for killing of one stag with a crossbow within Chadgley in his own land.

- One doe found killed by the wayside in Langden water, but we know not by whom.

- One deer killed within the tenement of Robert Rauthmell but we know not by whom.

- two stags found killed within Stoutt Close.

- one blind hind killed with a crossbow arrow.

- one deer killed with serving of the countes warrant of Yorke.

- Stephen Harrison of Batteres for felling 3 sapling stubs (added in small writing : Her Majesty's tenant, and for repair of his house.)

- George Harrison of Batteres for felling of 2 sapling stubs.

- the wife of Robert Parker of the Lees did find a pricke taken with a fallow dog and a black at the dry brook upon the Lees. (A pricket was a two-year-old buck.)

The last item is a report about the number of deer :
"A survey of the Queen's Majesty's game both of red and fallow deer taken the 21st day of September in the 36th year of the reign by view and survey of the keeper and tenants of the Forest, with tenants of Richard Houghton esquire, her Majesty's Steward and Officer within the Forest of Bouland, as also in Radham Parke, which are of all sorts both red and fallow deer, in the whole seven hundred or thereabout."

(Public Record Office, 1182, Duchy of Lancaster Special Commissions. D.L. 44, No. 520.)

The student of Bolland family names gets a rich harvest from the above pages. The old native Bolland name of Swinglehurst is found at Harden and Burholme. There are Parkers at Lickhurst, Sykes, Thorneyholm, Harden, Lees, and Graystonelee. Parkinsons are at Brennand and Woodhouse. Bleasdales are at Dinklingreen and Lees. There is a Sawer at Burholme and a Rudds or Rhodes at Stakes. The family names at Batteres are numerous : Stephen, George, and John Harrison, William Marton, Robert Bee, Alexander Turner. Another name of an unusual type is Henry Ballarde.

Names like Cottam, Dewhurst, and several others belong to the Chipping side and are not Bolland names. John Whippe seems to have been a servant of the Sherburns. Adam Holgate probably belonged to Bolland.

CHAPTER XIX.

CHIPPING PARISH AND BOLLAND FOREST.

The old register of baptisms, marriages, and burials, belonging to the parish of Chipping, has many references to places and persons of Bolland Forest. Naturally Leagrim and Little Bolland are more prominent than the rest, but the register contains numerous references to places in Great Bolland. Perhaps the most attractive of all the references is 1669, 28 March, Moses a child found within the forest of Bolland.

The chief Bolland names of places are Burholme, Dincklinge Greene (spelt also Inkelin Greene), Fayredock Houle (Farrick or Fair Oak), Fence, Graystonley, Harden, Leagrim, Lees, Lickhurst, Raddom Lawnde, Reed Barne (opposite Burholme), Saddle, Slaidburn, Stakes, and Wardesley (near Doeford Bridge).

1563 Rich Parker the sonne of Ranould Parker of Graystonlee in bolland nowe Viccar of Chippin et Scriptor hujus libri (Writer of this book) was christened.

1600 — Wilkinson s. of Jo. Wilkinson of Slaidburne

1601 Ellen pker als Salsburye the bastard daughter of James Salsbury of Chippin & — pker daughtr of old Arthure Parker Likehurst in Bolland

1601 Thomas Parker sonne of James pker of further Graystolye in Bolland was xxined at Chippin . . .

Mother of the said Thomas Parker was one Agnes Shereburne daughter of Mr. Robt. Shereburne of Woolffhall. (The writer then states that the infant was the first born of James and Agnes, then both aged 21, and that James was his cousin. The writer was the Vicar of Chipping. See above.)

The register has a very unusual Bolland name in the following: 1616 Janne prinit d. of Robt. prinit de Bolland.

The old Chipping family of Startivant, which gave its name to the farm now called Startifants, was represented at Lickhurst in 1654 when a John, son of Henry, was christened. The name Startivant is probably a Norman name and derives from Esterdevant—to be in front or in the vanguard.[1]

1655 Henrie s. of Robte Farrer of Bolland. The late Judge Farrer, a learned antiquarian, liked to trace his ancestry back to this family.

1656 Richard s. of Anthony Pooler of Bolland.

1660-1651 the family names of Bond, Barker, Marsden, and Wilkinson are mentioned.

[1] There are a number of Sterdevaunts in the U.S.A.

1668 John s. of John Dobson of New Lawnes in Bolland
Elizabeth d. of George Toulson of Stakes Esqr

Stakes Farm is a pleasant and solidly-built farm, with certain claims by its size and dignity to be called a gentleman's residence. It was probably built by the Richmond family, who must have had a certain standard of education in view of the Latin inscription on the wall that faces the Hodder :

Nunc mea
Mox hujus
Postea nescio cujus
Nemo sibi natus

A rough translation would be :

Now this is mine
Soon this other's
Afterwards whose I know not
Nobody is born for himself

It would be of interest to know why the owner of the house expressed himself in Latin. He may have felt that the rustics who could not read English need not be catered for, while any gentlemen who came that way would be duly impressed by the learned language on the house.

The Toulson family succeeded here by marriage an old yeoman family of Chipping, the Richmonds.

1669 Jenet d. of John Turner of Lickhurst in Bolland
Jenet d. of Thomas Pker of Whitewell in Bolland
Robt. s. of George Rauthmell of Bolland

1670 James s. of John Houle of Bolland

1671 Alice d. of Willm Sailsberie of Lickhurst in Bolland
Mary d. of Alexander Parker of Lickhurst in Bolland
Margret d. of Thomas Parker of Whitewell in Bolland
Susan d. of James Hannson of Bolland
John s. of George Rauthmell of Bolland

1673 Mary d. of John Dobson of Bolland
Ann d. of Richard Wignall of Bolland
Elizabeth d. of Willm Sailsberie of Lickhurst in Bolland
Mary d. of Thomas Parker of Whitewell in Bolland
Bridget d. of Alexander Parker of Lickhurst in Bolland.
Elizabeth d. of Thomas Hayes of Bolland

1674 Elizabeth d. of Christopher Sharpe of Bolland
Richard s. of George Rauthmell of Bolland
Margaret d. of James Hannson of Bolland
John s. of Thomas Badger of Bolland

1676 Henery s. of William Sailsberie of Lickhurst in Bolland
Margaret d. of Thomas Badger of Bolland
Renold s. of Thomas Parker of Whitewell in Bolland
Elin d. of Christopher Sharpe of Bolland

1677 Richard s. of Thomas Marsden of Lowd Mytham in Bolland

1678 Izabell d. of Robt. Dillworth of Bolland
Margaret d. of Roger Isherwood of Bolland

1679 Alis d. of Thomas Parker of Pimblins in Bolland
Robt. reputed sonn of John Parker of Lickhurst in Bolland

1680 John s. of Anthony Houson of Whitewell in Bolland
John s. of Robt Crosdell of Bolland
Alis d. of Thomas Parker of Bolland

1681 John s. of Robert Croosdell of Bolland
Henery s. of Richard Bleasdell in Bolland
Elizabeth d. of Christopher Sharpe of Bolland

1682 Elizabeth d. of Thomas Parker of Bolland

1683 Thomas s. of Richd. Dobson of Saddleside
Henery s. of Thomas Marsden of Bolland

1684 A bastard child of Willm Sailsberie of Bolland
Margaret d. of Rd Huson of Bolland
Margret d. of Thomas Parker of Bolland

1686 John s. of Thomas Parker of Bolland

1687 Hannah d. of Robert Crosdell of Bolland
Richard Housand s. of Richard Houson of Bolland

(The entry in 1684 Huson and the two spellings above show no doubt that the parson was trying to cope with an unfamiliar name.)

John s of Richard Bleasdaile of Bolland

BURIALS.

1600 Issabell Gregson alias Parker baste daughtr of Thomas Parker of Grastonlee fil Meg in Bolland being by misfortunate channce upon a heble[1] going over was drowned over a neede an ashe Beyond grastonlie my fatheres late howse for want of a good bridge and so carried downe to humfray linne[2] there found the same day being wensday the iii day of Septembr the ould bridge being driven dowen by a floode before.

(Within recent years two people have been drowned in the brooks that flow from the same fells. Normally a child could play in them but in flood they sweep all before them.)

[1] Heble is an interesting dialect word meaning a footbridge.

[2] Where is Humfray Linne ? Humphray Lumb is a pool in Greystoneley brook below the modern aqueduct. It is known to very few people today. The word *lumb* may be connected with the quarry nearby.

Ric Parker s of Thomas of Graistonlie
Edward Parker of Grastonlee

(There were, therefore, three funerals from Graystonelee in 1600.)

1601 Edward Coulthurst of Wardesley

1616 Henrie Bleasdale of Incklen greene

1622 Thomas Pker of Lickhurst

1623 Widow Swinlehurst of Burhoulme
A childe of Widdowe Swinlehursts

(The years 1622 and 1623 record an extraordinary number of deaths, especially of children. Whereas a normal year in the register only occupies part of a page, these years have over three pages. The deaths of some 40 children are recorded at this time and the following year 1624 is equally full, although the register is incomplete here.)

1627 James Parker son of Robert Parker of Leekehurst in Bolland

1633 John Bleasdall of Inckelingreene

1653 Agnes d. of Robert Marsden of Bolland

1654 Ann Bostock of Bolland

1655 Henry Bleasdall of Incleinge Green in Bolland.
Alexander Bleasdall of Incleinge Green

1657 The wife of Thomas Wilcock of Raddom Lawnd
Henry Charpeles of Borholme

1660 James Parker of Higher Grastone Lee
Renald Parker of Lower Grastone Lee

1661 A childe of Robert Farrar of Bolland
Richard Hughson of Dinckley Green

1667 The wife of Thomas Bond of Burholme
John s. of Anne Bisbrowne of Bolland
Renald Parker of Whitewell in Bolland

1668 Henerie s. of Robt Farrar Graistonlee in Bolland
Thomas Willcocke of Lees in Bolland
Henerie Charnocke of Bolland Shoomaker
A childe of Christopher Swinglehurst of Borholme

1669 John Dobson of New Lawnes in Bolland
The wife of John Bond in Bolland
The wife of John Bond of Borholme
Isabell Toulson Ant to George Toulson of Stakes Gentleman
John Parker of Lickhurst in Bolland Senior

1670 Margret d. of Phillipp Walker of Burholme
Thomas s. of Robert Farrand in Bolland

1671 Thomas s. of Robt Dobson of Whitewell in Bolland
Henerie s. of Henerie Kighley of Bolland
Widow Pker of Grastonly in Bolland
John s. of Alexander Parker of Lickhurst In Bolland

1672 Alexander s. of Thomas Bond of Burholme.
Willm Parker of Lickhurst in Bolland
Bridget d. of Alexander Parker of Lickhurst in Bolland

1673 Elizabeth w. of John Parker of Bolland
Elizabeth d. of Robt Farrand of Bolland
The wife of Roger Parker of Graystonlee in Bolland

1674 The wife of Thomas Parker of Greystonlee in Bolland
Henery s. of Christopher Sower of Bolland
John Bradley of Bolland
Widow Charnocke of Bolland
Elizabeth Sharpe of Burholme

1675 Hnery Parker of Pimblines[1] in Bolland
Thomas s. of Bartholomew Fairclough of Bolland

1676 The wife of Robt. Rauthmell of Lees in Bolland
Henery Knowles of Harden in Bolland
John Dobson of Reed Barne in Bolland

1677 A child of Robt Dillworth of Bolland
Alexander Parker of Lickhurst in Bolland
Reynard Sharples of Bolland
Jenet d. of Richard Marsden of Gibbon Bridge in Bolland

1678 Henery s. of John Bleasdell of Dincklinge Greene in Bolland
Margret w. of John Harrison of Bolland

1679 Robt Rawthmell of Lees in Bolland
A child of Wm Sailsberies of Lickhurst in Bolland
Elizabeth w. of Willm Sailsberie of Lickhurst in Bolland
Alis d. of Thomas Parker of Pimblins in Bolland
John s. of Christopher Swinglehurst of Burholme

1680 Richard Bond of Bolland
Jennat Thorntan widdow of Bolland

1681 Thomas Boulton of Bolland
Robt son of Arthur Rawthmell of Bolland
Thomas Parker of Graistinley in Bolland
Mathew s. of James Parker of Bolland
Thomas Boulton of Bolland

1682 Thomas Bleasdell of Bolland
A child of Susan Butterfield of Bolland
Margrett d. of Thomas Marsden of Loudmithonn
Margrett Wright of Bolland

[1] *Pimblines* is near Lower Greystonely.

1683 A child of Richd Farrars of Bolland
Mary w. of Christopher Sharpe of Bolland
Margret Wignall of Bolland

1684 Elizabeth w. of Richd Farrar of Bolland
Margert d. of Richd Farrer of Bolland
Ann Banaster of Bolland
Richard Staning of Bolland

1685 A child of Robt. Crosedaile of Bolland

1686 Bartholomey Faireclough of Bolland

MARRIAGES.

1656 John Norcrosse of Bolland Hatmaker and Margret Cowell of Preston.

1669 John Dillworth of Dinklinge Greene in Bolland and Jenet Bond of Borholme in Bolland

1679 Thomas Poomfret of Blackburne and Elizabeth Pooler of Bolland

1684 Richard Haighton of Cheaghley and Grace Haythornethwaite of Bolland

1686 Richd Dobson of Chippin and Ann Dillworth of Bolland
John Clayton of Greenfold in the parish of Slaidburn and Ann Boulton of Chipping
Alexander Parke of Bolland and Ann Bradley
Richd Parker of Goosnargh and Ann Parker of Bolland
Henry Marsden and Isabel Guy both of Bolland
Thomas Eliot and Ann Fowler both of Bolland

* * * *

The Chipping Register is an interesting and unusual witness for the bad weather during the summer of 1600. On the second page of the fly-sheet is written : Between Pendle and Pirelook (Parlick) two knowne hills there was not three fare dayes in all in sixe weeks last before the sixt of Octobr above said, and six weeks before to the great loss of much corne : being great showe on the grounde.

The twelve weeks of bad weather here recorded as happening before the sixth of October mean that from the middle of July (otherwise St. Swithun's day) there was the legendary rain.

CHAPTER XX.

THE FOREST IN THE REIGN OF CHARLES II.

The Yorkshire part of Bolland Forest remained part of the Crown lands until Charles II. When this monarch was restored to the throne in 1660, it was chiefly through the authority of General Monk, who instead of making himself a military dictator like Cromwell, decided to restore the exiled King. Charles II rewarded the General in many ways, creating him Duke of Albemarle and endowing him with various possessions. One such proud gift was the ancient and royal Forest of Bolland.

In the deeds and archives of the Honour of Clitheroe preserved at Clitheroe Castle there is a most interesting old parchment from the days of Charles II, which is a survey of Bolland Forest for the information of its new lord, the Duke of Albemarle. The document tells us most of the old names of farms and grazings, and in some cases gives us the names of tenants. The smallness of the rents would amaze some of the tenants of the present day.

The following are the principle parts of this ancient parchment. It is first declared that in the Forest there are a Court Leet, a Court Baron, a Woodmote, and Swainmote, held twice a year for the Forest at the Lodge of Whitewell, Yorkshire. The Lancashire parts of the Forest of Little Bolland owe suit and service to these courts. These four courts were really all part of the same lawful government and authority in the Forest. The first two—Court Leet and Court Baron—are Norman names, while the last two—Woodmote and Swainmote—are Saxon. They all existed to safeguard in various ways the rights and privileges of the Lord of the Manor and to punish acts of theft, poaching, and trespass. The fact that two Norman names of courts are superimposed on two Saxon names shows how the feudal system of the Normans was grafted on to the earlier government of the English.

The chief officers of these courts were two Bowbearers appointed by the Lord of the Manor. Various estates and rents are now listed :—

	£	s.	d.
N.B. vaccary generally means stock-farm.			
Harrop and Nettlecarr pasture and vaccary	6		
Harcroft pasture and turbary (turf-cutting)		6	8
Gregston Legh vaccary	4	0	0
Brentslack pasture and vaccary (Burnslack)	1	1	8
Beatrix pasture and vaccary	5	8	6
Beatrix vaccary	1	1	8

(Batrrix was clearly an important stock-rearing farm. A local tradition says that markets were sometimes held there.)

Leigh House vaccary	1	9	0
(This farm is no doubt today represented by Lower, Middle and Higher Lees near Whitewell.)			
Thorneyholme pasture and vaccary	1	14	
Fairdockhouse (Farrick) vaccary	4	11	8
Ashknott and Dinkley Green vaccaries	3	12	8
Leekhurst vaccary and Crosdale Score pasture	4	12	8
Byerholme vaccary (Burholme)	7	4	
Trough and Sikes vaccaries	6	6	8
Haresden vaccary	5	16	9
Staple Oak vaccary	3	10	4
Gradall and Highokehill	5		
(Gradall, as pointed out elsewhere, lies by Merrybent farm higher up the Hodder than Slaidburn.)			
Korlowe pastures	11	10	

(A note in the margin says "or Horlow". It would seem likely that the clerk writing out the parchment was trying to read somebody else's writing. Could this be Catlow pastures? As Rawmoor is not mentioned, and as it lies closer to Gradall than Catlow, could this be Rawmoor?)

	£	s.	d.
Fishery in Bolland	11	6	8
Market	1	17	10½

(We are not told who had the rights of fishing in Bolland, which brought in quite a substantial sum. No doubt the Hodder was teeming with trout, grayling, and salmon in the days before the industries injured fishing. The present writer remembers as a boy seeing salmon three feet long lying dead in the Hodder.

We are not told where the market was held. At the time of writing, this has not been identified. A possible place is the one already mentioned at Battrix, even though its remoteness makes it seem unlikely, but Slaidburn would be a more obvious place. However, as the Forest court was then held at Whitewell, the market may have been in the same place.)

	£	s.	d.
Demesne of Slaidburn called Butterfield near Crosdale and Baxwell Flat	1	13	8
Demesne of Slaidburn called Hall Flat	2	13	8
Admarsh Mill		6	8
Long Knott	1	2	7

Demesne Estates.

	£	s.	d.
Radholme Lawn			
Wardsley	17	15	0
Lees Pasture, New Launds and			
Whitmore Knotts	36	13	8

(These estates around Whitewell were obviously good lands that brought in high rents. No rent is mentioned for Radholme Lawn probably because one of the Forest officers was in charge there.)

	£	s.	d.
Part of Lees Pasture	12	5	
ditto	12	5	
ditto	18	12	6
remainder of ditto	23	10	
Fence Tenement	40		
Part of Stott Heys Pastures	5	2	6
other part thereof	5	2	6
other 2 parts thereof	10	5	

(The Stott Heys or Stud Close pastures were situated by the Hodder opposite Burholme. Hodder Bank farm today will contain most of the above lands.)

	£	s.	d.
Whitedale	18		
Brenand pasture	18	8	6
Part of late Parkinson's Tenement	6	5	½
remainder of ditto	6	5	½

These tenements would probably be near Dunsop Bridge.

	£	s.	d.
Old Farme	11	5	3
Long Knot	9		

(Where is Old Farm?)

* * *

Ancient Rights and Dues

A Court Baron is held every three weeks at Slaidburn to deal with actions of less than ten shillings.

The Liberty of Bolland comprises the townships of Slaidburn, Newton, Easington, Grindleton, Bradford cum Waddington, Mitton cum Bashall, Bolland cum Legrim.

The Manor of Slaidburn . . . . . Freehold rent

		Freehold rent
Bashall	Wm Walmsley Esq.	£8 10 7¼
	Toddreel Esq.	£8 7 8
The Manor of Mitton	Heirs of Sir Walter Hawksworth	£8 7 8
Withgill	Ed. Tildesley	£8 7 8
Battersby Hall		pair of gloves
Chapel Croft		pound of pepper

Rents.

——	Thos. Wittam	5s
Hollins	Adam Hatkill	2s
Knot Gate	Jn Parsons	1s
——	Robt. Hide	2s3d
Standris	Thos. Cave	1d
Essington	Nic. Banister	1s
——	Ed. Wikshall	
Rents in Newton		
Ed. Hodgkinson		7d
Ralph Faber		7d

(End of the document.)

The Withgill demesne held by Edward Tyldesley included the ancient part of Mitton parish known as Crook, from the crooked course of the Hodder below Hodder bridge. The farmland of Sagar Fold, which derived its name from the occupiers of it in the eighteenth century, is part of the same estate.

Battersby Hall is the original name of Dunnow. At this date it was no longer held by the Battersby family.

A remarkable fact about these ancient rents is that Chapel Croft should only pay a pound of pepper. The reason for this has not been ascertained.

The parchment from which the above is copied was dated 1662. There is also a copy at the Castle dated 1735.

Knollmere, or Knowlmere, family home for the Peels. The family and the house are part of the community structure of the area.

CHAPTER XXI.

THE FOREST BOUNDS IN THE 17th CENTURY.

Whitaker's *History of Whalley* quotes from an old survey of the Forest boundaries, which he dates from the early part of the seventeenth century. There is a reference in the deed to "the grounds of Clem. Towlson"—this would be the land at Stakes occupied by Captain Clement Townson from about 1640 to the end of the century, and so the survey is probably later than Whitaker suggests.

The attempt to retrace the old boundary line and to identify some of the old names has been a fascinating task. It has involved many long journeys, many interviews and questionings with oldest inhabitants and dwellers in remote places. It has involved many false tracks and many disappointments, but it has also provided many thrills and many happy discoveries.

It may be best to repeat the description of the boundary section by section, and to discuss the identification of each part in the process.

"Beginning at the lowe end of Graddell and adjoining to a certayn place called Grange." How many people in Bolland today could describe where to find the low end of Graddell adjoining to a certain place called Grange? Graddell is one of the old Bolland names that deserves to be preserved because Graddell moor was at one time an extensive grazing ground for the Slaidburn district. It lies between Croasdale and the upper Hodder. Grange—often called Rushton Grange—was an old and important farmstead, which now lies under the water of the Stocks-in-Bolland reservoir. The nearness of the Grange to the river explains why the boundary begins at "the low end of Graddell", showing that it is in the valley.

The boundary line goes on : "and soe along after a river called Hodder, leading to Cross of Greate, which bounds north-east upon the lordship of Horneby". The splendid massiveness of the cross-base is still there to mark the site of Cross of Greet, above where Hodder rises. Even today when it can be reached by car, it is still possible to catch some of the past importance of such a boundary mark, when it towered alone above the sweep of the fells and was rarely visited even by the few shepherds who lived in this remote and secluded wilderness.

"As heaven water deales, and from thence to Croasdale and Whitledale." The following of the watershed—"as heaven water deals"—is very common in the description of old boundaries. The boundary line in this area follows the division between Lancashire and Yorkshire, the Lancashire line being the old boundary of the manor of Hornby. Today there is no trace of the old cross at the head of Whitendale, which is mentioned in the old Hornby records published by Colonel Chippendall.[1]

"And part of Brennand North, which bounds upon said lordship of Horneby, as heaven water deales."

"The rest is from Brennand, and bounds upon the farmers of Tarnebrooke, and so to a place called Ughtersik, as Harrington ditch leads, lying over the west end of Millhouse."

Brennand, Tarnbrook, and Millhouse are all on the ordnance map. But what of Ughtersik—a very unusual name—and of Harrington ditch ? After long and troublesome enquiries, it was found that the only people who had ever heard of Ughtersik were some old farmers at Tarnbrook. They eventually decided that Ughtersik was what they called *Oosterset*, a landmark high up on the fells, not far from the other landmark called Millhouse or Millers House. Later it was discovered that Teesdale's map of Lancashire (1828) marks Oughter Side where the more recent maps place Millers House. If the older reading Ughtersik is more correct the name would refer to the name of a stream or sike. Actually the farm of Sykes is in the valley not far away.

The Harrington ditch must have been a more notable landmark in the Middle Ages and later centuries than at the present, just as in the same way it is probable that Mill House probably looked more like what its name implies than it does today. The story of how Harrington Dike or Ditch was at last found is told in another chapter.

"And so as heaven water deales, over the Threape Hawe to the stone in the Trough that divides Yorkshire from Lancashire." This is the line of the county boundary today.

"And from thence west from Sykes, which bounds upon Marshay, Hathernwaite, Catshay, Calder, Bleasdale, Fairsnape, Blindhurst, and Wolfhall, as heaven water divides."

The speed at which the boundary-makers travel along the fell-tops as heaven water divides, passing from the Trough to the fells above Chipping, shows that this moorland was uncharted and unclaimed. Even today it only supports a few sheep and a few grouse. The boundary descends to more populated and more cultivated land as it approaches the Leagrim estate.

"And from thence down brooke called Dobson Brooke to Chippin Brooke and so all along after by the ende of Chippin towne, and about 16 roodes downe brooke of Chippin, and so lineally to Red Banke."

1 This must have been one of the most isolated wayside crosses in England.

All the above except Red Banke are to be found on the modern map.

"And from thence all along the lands of Richard Marsden of the Pale, which bounds part upon Mr. Yates his grounds, the lordship of Thorneley and lordship of Braidley Hall."

"And from thence to after the grounds of Clem. Towlson, bounding upon the lordship of Braidley Hall aforesaid."

If the interpretation of the above is correct, the boundary follows the line of Chipping Brook to the Loud, and so to the Hodder.

"Then after, and all along the grounds of Rob. Rawthmell, bounding upon Mr. Shereburne lordship and Mr. Sunderland lordship. Thence to Wyerburne Foot, Browsholme, and Newhay, bounds upon the lordship of Bashall."

The Rawthmell mentioned above was probably at Wardsley, opposite to Stakes. The Shereburne lordship would no doubt be the adjoining Leagrim estate which extends as far as Loud Mytham and Doeford Bridge.

The name Wyerburne seems to have been lost and is no doubt represented by the Mill brook which rises near Browsholme and flows into Hodder.

As explained in an earlier chapter on boundaries, Newhay is the old name for the estate below Waddington fell and above the village of Waddington. This fits in with the general line of the boundary, which is now climbing up to Waddington fell and to the heights leading back towards the starting point on the upper reaches of the Hodder.

"Thence over common called Whitstoncliff, Bradford Moore, and Grinleton Moore, which bounds south upon lordship of Waddington, and the coppie-houlders of Bradford and Grinleton, parcel of manor of Slaydburne."

The copy-hold tenants of Waddington, West Bradford, and Grindleton had been among the first to encroach upon the forest where it used to be bounded by the Ribble. They had gradually pushed back the forest boundary towards the hill-tops.

"And lastlie, thence to Vaccary of Harrope, within forest of Bolland, which bounds upon south-east side of lordship of Boulton."

The boundary does not seem complete, as it ought to have mentioned Champion, but Slaidburn and the Hammerton Hall estate around it have long ceased to be counted as part of Bolland Forest.

CHAPTER XXII.

HARRINGTON DIKE—AN OLD LANDMARK IN BOLLAND.

These notes would have been headed "The oldest landmark in Bolland," were it not that the ancient cross-stump of massive grey granite, which stands by the source of the Hodder at Cross of Greet, can probably claim to be Bolland's oldest landmark. Yet Harrington Dike must be a good rival in age, as it is probably some 500 if not 600 years old.

What is Harrington Dike and where is it ? Harrington Dike is an old boundary ditch running between the domains of Hornby and Bolland. As its name implies, it was marked out by the Harringtons, who were lords of Hornby towards the end of the Middle Ages. Whitaker's *History of Whalley* states that traces of this dike could be seen on the tops of the fells between the Trough and Cross of Greet, that is where the old boundary would run part of the way, and where the present boundary between Lancashire and Yorkshire still marks some of the same division.

Starting with the statement by Whitaker that some traces of the Harrington Dike could still be found, the present writers set off to discover it for themselves. An approach was made more than once from the Trough road and several miles of the wild moorland searched for any trace of a ditch or boundary embankment. Shepherds and farmers were asked if they had heard of Harrington Dike. This question must have been asked dozens of times in the Hodder Valley and in the Trough region, even beyond the Trough, around Quernmore and Tarnbrook. Invariably the answer was that nobody had heard about Harrington Dike.

Then the next question was if any ditch or embankment existed on the tops of the fells. An old shepherd living at Sikes was the only person who considered that there might have been an old ditch above where Whitendale and Croasdale met, close to the old road from Croasdale. Twice this place was approached on foot from Croasdale, but nothing was found. Once an attempt was made from out of the Brennand Valley, climbing up to the tops towards Miller House, but again nothing was discovered.

A clue that was to prove of very real help was found in an old document from the Hornby estate. In 1939 Colonel W. H. Chipindall had published a *Survey of the Hornby Castle Estates* (Chetham Society) and his book reprinted certain old descriptions of the various boundaries. One document described the Boundaries of Roeburndale (spelt Robrondale) and mentioned an old ditch at the top of Whitendale.

This could only be the Harrington Dike without the name, and so the account given of it was studied very carefully. The following is a quotation of the part about Harrington Dike :

"So ascending Northward as the same ditch goeth to Whitledale Cross, and so turning westward along the same old ditch dividing Roborondale and Botton to the Brown Hill, and so following along the same ditch westward to the East end of Hawkshead, and thence descending northward to the said ditch to Thursgill Stoop . . ."[1]

All these places are easy to find on a map—Whitendale, Roeburndale, Botton, Hawshead, and Thrushgill. Unfortunately there is no trace today of Whitendale Cross, which must have stood there at the top of the valley, rather like the Cross of Greet, and nobody in the district can remember any remains of a cross in that lonely part of the fells.

In view of the mention of Botton and Thrushgill by the old document, an attempt was made to find the Dike from that side. The approach was made from near where the Manchester Corporation has its new tunnel, and incidentally from where the Roman road begins to climb the fells towards Bolland.

From Thrushgill the slope towards Hawkshead was climbed and in the distance a long dark line, too straight to be a natural landmark, slowly became more visible, marking its way along the side of the fell. The east end of Hawkshead is certainly one of the best places to discover the old ditch, and from there it can be followed with ease, either towards Whitendale or in the opposite direction above Thrushgill.

If it followed the line of the watershed, it would look like a wide drainage ditch, but it makes no attempt to follow the lie of the land. It is clearly a boundary ditch or foss.

Owing to the thick growth of bent and heather, it is easy to lose the Dike as it approaches Whitendale, and the reason why it could not easily be discovered when approached from that side was obvious. If the reader would like to trace out for himself the centuries-old and almost forgotten line of Harrington Dike, he is recommended to start from the east end of Hawkshead.

Incidentally, some of the farmers around Thrushgill and Botton seem to know of the old ditch, not as Harrington Dike, but as the "Mill Race." However, the idea of a mill race there can be dismissed as merely a modern attempt to account for the strange ditch made so long ago by the Harringtons of Hornby.

[1] Thrushgill today.

CHAPTER XXIII.

KNOLLMERE.

The early history of the estate has been studied in the chapter on the Hamerton family. Miss Peel printed for private circulation a short history called *The Manor of Kowlmere.*[1] The book contains some information that might have been lost and contains descriptions of unusual features at various farms on the estate. Some of her gleanings about Chapelcroft will be found under that heading.

After the execution of Sir Stephen Hamerton, Knollmere remained in the possession of the Crown until the first year of the reign of Philip and Mary. The estate was then presented to Cuthbert Musgrave and his heirs male to be held by knight's service. This was a reward for services in Scotland.[2]

Cuthbert Musgrave died at Richmond, Yorkshire, on 23rd September 1592, being succeeded by his son Cuthbert. The legal deposition after death mentions his Knowllmere possessions as follows : Fowlskales, Yolstones, Knollstanes, Knollsawe, Mosthwait, Lagher Thornholme, Hundell, Marlehill, Whithellhouse, Mennelaine, and Surefield ; 4 messuages in Knollmyer in the tenure of Richard Lee, Stephen Raude, Adam Turner, and Robert Proctor ; a cottage in the tenure of George Dodgson, two cottages called Orchen Streete and Rugge House, a messuage and a close called Heshnesthey.[3]

Most of these names have been discussed in the Hamerton chapter. The Orchen Streete of this document takes on a different appearance from the Orchenstrett of Henry VIII's time. If we knew that this house was situated near the old Roman road as it passes through Knollmere, we could safely say that the Streete was a reference to the road. However, for want of further evidence, it is only a surmise.

In 1661 Charles II gave a royal licence to William Musgrave, enabling him to convey Knollmere to Sir G. Fletcher, who was about to marry his niece, Lady Mary Graham. In the following century an Act was passed in 1769 allowing Sir Bellingham Graham to transfer the property to Sir J. K. Lister, Bt., and William Weddell, Esq. Two years later the property was sold to John Lyon and Wm. Turner, bankers of Nottingham. From these the property was bought in 1805 by Jonathan Peel of Accrington House, Lancs.

1 Preston, 1913.

2 Peel, p. 13.

3 Not in Peel but from Court of Wards, *Inquisit post mortem*, vol. 24, fol. 7.

To judge from the description given by Miss Peel of the site of old farmsteads near Knollmere, there was almost a small village in this part of the valley. All these farms have disappeared. There was one by the Hipping Stones. On the north of the present house there was another, and also a farm called Greygill between Knollmere and Mossthwaite.

Chapelcroft.

In the Hamerton chapter the question of Chapelcroft was discussed and its existence proved in the Middle Ages. Miss Peel in her Knollmere history suggests that there was once a chapel on this site. She writes : "My father showed me the bases of the pillars (as he thought) or buttresses at regular distances in the turf of the croft."[1] And later : "That there was a burial ground attached is almost certain, for besides my remembrance of the tradition, old Rushton and his wife Mary (formerly M. Isherwood) told us when Nina and Eleanor, our nieces, took us to see them, that in the Brocklehurst's time and before the Isherwoods, who farmed there about 1830-1840, two or three large gravestones were visible near the garden wall and still uncovered with turf."[2]

Over the house door there is carved IP EP 1669, and on the barn IP GP 1691. There is some kind of unusual stone in the bridge over the stream nearby. Miss Peel calls it a window-head.

SLIM ROW (SLAMEMORROW) AND YOULSTONWOOD.

There are a number of vanished names and places in Bolland —among them are Slamemorrow and Youlstonwood.[3] Slamemorrow was sometimes written Slamerow ; part of it survives today as Slim Row. Youlstonwood seems to have been another farming colony in the neighbouring region of Bonstone Wood.

In the period 1600-1700, when the upper Hodder valley seems to have been more prosperous and more thickly populated than at any time of its history, there must have been quite a number of small farmers at places like Slim Row and Youlstonwood. Lower Slim Row is now falling into ruin. A doorway over the middle dwelling has the date 1665. Some of it is made of what is called locally "white sandstone"—a name that brings meaning to the landmark Whitstonecliff, on the fells not far away. There are several enclosed gardens, and one of the disused enclosures is called the Wellhole. According to an old tradition the middle dwelling was at one time a Dame school.

[1] p. 47.
[2] p. 48.
[3] Youlstone probably means Old Stone.

A thoughtful photographer wrote the date - April 21st 1905 - on this sample of his work. The group look handsomely dressed outside a house in Church Street, Slaidburn. The Rectory is in the background and the two pillars stand at the entrance to Tithebarn Yard. In later years the house would become well-known as an ice cream shop.

Looking towards the village centre. To the right of the large tree is a lamp post. On this spot the Slaidburn War Memorial would be erected soon after 1918. Just out of sight on the left is the Girls' School, which was set up in the 1870s and merged with Brennands Boys' School about 1904.

The sturdy building on the left just past the green, a piece of common land long used for grazing, is the Methodist Chapel, paid for by local people in the 1820s and refurbished about 1889.

Looking out of Slaidburn with the village green on the right. The building at the far end of the row is a joiner's shop. On the extreme left is a wheelbarrow specially designed to carry peat.

According to the old Slaidburn Court rolls, one of the principal families here in the seventeenth century bore the name of Walne.

Richard Walne passed a holding at Youlstonewood to his son Nicholas 1672.

Robert Wallbank passed land at Slamemorrow to Nicholas Walne 1676.

Nicholas Walne and his wife passed land at Slamemorrow to Wm Birket, 1682.

The Register of Waddington church, which is now published, mentions several Bolland families, including that of Walne, sometimes spelt Wawne. The Walne family must have been in this same district for many generations because the earliest reference found is a suit in Slaidburn Court Rolls—James Parker v. Robert Parker of Chapelcroft and Nicholas Walne (26 Henry VIII, 1535-1536).

When investigations were taking place into the existence of an old chapel at Burholme, some local people suggested that if it had existed it must have been a Quaker meeting room. The origin of this idea was that American Quakers of the name of Walne claimed that their ancestors lived at Burholme. Excavations indicated that the chapel at Burholme was probably medieval and not just a meeting room. (See the chapter on Burholme chapel).

However a curious and faded inscription at Burholme was pointed out set in the wall of an outbuilding, and this was supposed to be a religious inscription. The stone seems to read as follows :

I JANE LOVE FOR TRU
TO W// AN / FAITH
FUL I WIL BE

There was a Jane Walne baptised at Waddington in 1647, and a Janet Wilkinson described as of Burham baptised in 1631 ; she was the daughter of Edmund Wilkinson, who died 1638. It is possible that the Burholme stone may refer to one or the other, but apart from its profession of love and fidelity, its significance is unknown.[1]

The chief family names before 1700 in Slim Row and Youlstonewood were : Hairst, Wallbank, Hodgkinson, Parker, Marsden, Parkinson, Scott, Swinglehurst, Standen, Sharples, Stackhouse, Fort, Bleazard, Graham, Turner, Raingill, Harrison and Birket. The most typical names of the district are underlined.

Further information can be found in the unpublished Slaidburn Register and the unpublished and numerous volumes of the Slaidburn Court Rolls.

[1] See Chapter XIX marriage of Jenet Bond, 1669.

STAKES.

The name of this old farm is unusual and not easy to explain. If it had been near the boundary of one of the deer-parks it might have been named after where there was a staked fence, but this explanation is unlikely. A document from Cromwell's time gives an account of the fields and buildings belonging to Stakes and may contain a clue to the name.

According to this survey, the land just around Stakes was called the Warth, and on this piece of land was a house called Stakes, "with a fair garden adjoining", and also a house of stone called the Boathouse. It is tempting to surmise that there was once a rough kind of wharf here and that the Stakes were mooring posts or guide-posts for boats. Certainly the mention of the stone Boathouse reveals a state of affairs that has no resemblance with conditions today, when there is no memory of a Boathouse, not to mention a boat. Of course it is only in flood-time that the Hodder has anything approaching the former flow of water, because the river is heavily tapped by three thirsty enterprises—the upper Hodder is drained by Blackpool and Fleetwood, the Brennand and Whitendale are drained by Blackburn, and the Langden is drained by Preston. In an earlier age a boat was no doubt often useful, but today the nearest boat to Hodder is Hacking boat just below the Hodder's flow into Ribble.

In 1613 there was a royal Commission[1] concerning a complaint by Henry Richmond of Stakes against Henry Clarke and Thomas Turner. Henry Richmond was tenant by lease from the Crown and the matter in dispute was about rights of felling trees and clearing ground—stubbing and grubbing. We gather that various trees had been removed—oak, ash, birch, oller and wicken (alder and willow)—and that on the Lees one of the best coverts for game had been damaged.

James Parker of the Lees in Bolland stated that tenants had power to stub and grub by their leases. It seems clear that such a power became the death-warrant of the Forest, because it opened the door to wholesale unlicensed clearings. The amount of encroachment throughout the years, in the name of better husbandry, must have been tremendous. The same James Parker says that Thomas Turner removed 8 sapling oaks from Bolland to Bashall Eaves to a place called Horsehey, and that he stubbed in Dawe Wood, Ruffawe near Raddom Park side 14 acres.

That evidence is typical of the encroachments that had been gradually since the Middle Ages.

[1] Duchy of Lancaster Depositions, I James II, Bundle 61, no. 42.

The Chipping Register has some information on Stakes (see separate chapter) and we see how Clement Toulson came to Stakes through his marriage to Mary Richmond. A report in the Public Record Office from 1655 gives a very full description of all the Stakes buildings and fields. Instead of entering into all the details of this document the field names will be quoted from it. Where a name is marked *, this means that it has been identified at Stakes by the present dwellers there.

One house in the Newlands called the Newlands House with a barn and garden about 3 roods.

A piece of arable land called Clayholme.
A piece of meadow called Shrubbs.*
A piece of meadow called the meadow.
A piece of pasture called the Newlands.
A piece of arable called the inclosed Lawne.
A piece of pasture called the Horse Hole.
A piece of meadow called the Scarholme.
A piece of pasture called the Stubbed Close.*
A piece of pasture called the Dawholme.*
A piece of woodland called Dawood.*
A piece of meadow called Dawholme.*
A piece of pasture called the Lordship.*
A piece of mossland called the Playne.
A piece of pasture called the Norwood.
A piece of pasture part arable and part meadow called Swannyholme.*
A piece of pasture called Calf Parrock.
A piece of pasture called Whitmore Knott.
A piece of land called the Warth.
A house called the Stakes with a fair garden adjoining.
A piece of arable called the Holme.*
A piece of meadow called the Meadow on the back of the house.*
A piece of arable called the Little Marled Field.
A piece of arable called the Buckplace.
A piece of meadow called the Great Marled Close.
A piece of meadow called the Scarholme.
A piece of woodland called the Scar.
A piece of land called the Warth and a house of stone therein erected with a place called the Boathouse.[1]

[1] Chancery Proceedings before 1714, Mitford 127—147.

CHAPTER XXIV.

SOME BOLLAND WILLS.

To study all the wills registered from Bolland would need a book in itself. The following selection has been chosen more or less at random from the old wills that were formerly registered at Richmond, and form part of the York records. Some of the very oldest wills, the earliest dated 1407, were specially chosen to see how far the old wills were in any respect different from those of later generations.

It is no doubt probable that a more complete study of the old wills would reveal a number of informative items. The present small selection is instructive in several ways. The oldest wills have not only bequests to monasteries, no doubt to ask for the usual spiritual favours granted to all benefactors, but they contain such public-spirited bequests as :

for the building of the church tower at Slaidburn
for a new bridge over the Lune at Lancaster
for a new bridge over the Hodder at Slaidburn

The people of those days seem to have been conscientious bridge-builders and to have treated the work as an act of piety—hence the ancient bridge-chapels such as those preserved still at Rotherham and Wakefield, and the old wayside cross on the old Hodder bridge at Slaidburn, the stump of which is still by the side of the present bridge, and built into it.

A very long will of John Guy, dated June 11th 1644, is quite out of the ordinary and shows that he was a money-lender. It is not included because it contains too many names not of Bolland.

SKYPSE, Richard, Rector of Slaidburn 3 Ides of November 1402

He is to be buried in the cemetery of St. Andrew's church near the entrance by the north part.

To my mother 10£ To Robt. Skypse all my books and 100s.
To Thomas my kinsman 100s and a bed

Benefactions to Richard the cook, Laurence, Thomas, my page. Heliseus Parker, Richard Patsyn, Dominus Richard the Clerk, Alice the daughter of Nicholas
2 beams for the Croasdale bridge
Residue to Thomas Semer (Seymour?) and Hugh Paitsyn,
Executors Christopher Batersby.

Note. The legacies to Richard the cook, Laurence, and Thomas the page, indicate probably the domestic helpers of the Rector. It is a pity that we have none of the recipes of Richard the cook.

. . . .

In some of the following wills there are bequests to the Brothers of Lancaster—the Blackfriars or Dominicans ; to the

Brothers of Preston—the Greyfriars or Friars Minor ; the Brothers of Appleby—the White Friars or Carmelites ; and the Cistercians of Kirkstall and Sallay are also mentioned.

BOND : JOHN DE SYKES Date : 10th October, 1407

Chaplain to celebrate in chapel in 'Wyresdale'
Margaret Langta.
William Clag(h)ton—
John, son of Nicholas Bond.
John Kamp.
Robert, son of Nicholas
William, son of ? (next line starts medit-medicus?)
John Langta
Richard Langta.
Daughter of Thomas Bond.
Thomas Bond.
John de Blesedale
John Bond.
Katerine, my daughter.
Daughters of William Whittyngdale
and Katerin, his wife—viz:
Isabelle and Lisote.
Executors : Nicholas, my son. Richard, my son. Thomas, my son.

JOHN BOND (additional)

To the Brothers of Lancaster, Preston, Appleby and Augustinians of York. Two marks to be divided amongst them.

WHITTLEDALE. Henry de. Date : 30.Oct. 1428.

Bur in Slatburn—near "William my son"
xls to the building of Church Tower (Campanile) at Slaidburn.
Executors—Elizabeth my wife.
William de Oxcliff.
Witnesses—Magister William de Newerk. Rector.
Nicholas de Mandesley. Chaplain.
Given at my house in Bolland.
To the Brothers of Lancaster and the Convent there, 6s.8d.
To the Brothers and Convent of Preston. 6s.8d.

HOLDEN, Henry de.
Date: Monday before feast of Simon and Jude, 1429.

Buried in cemetery of Church of "Slaytburn'.

Item lego facture nom pontem lapidi altea aquam de Luene apud Lancastre. 3s.4d. for new bridge over the Lune at Lancaster.

To Thomas de Maudisley, chaplain, to celebrate—7 marks.

To making a church tower of Slaytburn, VIs.VIIId.
To Nicholas de Maudisley, chaplain, XIId.
To William de Middlebroke, clerk, VId.
Residue after Charitable bequests for dowry of three unmarried, unnamed daughters.

Executors : Margaret—my wife.
Robert & John. her sons.
Rector : Supervisor.
Witnesses : William de Mewerk, rector.
Thomas de Maudisley, chaplain.
Reg. Ebor. II. 663 6.

To Abbot and Convent of 'Crestall' (Kirkstall?)	VIs.VIIId.
To Abbot and Convent of Sallay	VIs.VIIId.
To Friars Minor of Preston	VIs.VIIId.
To Friars Preachers of Lancaster	VIs.VIIId.

BUTTERFIELD, JOHN. Date : 16 May, 1440

To Thomas Richemond, chaplain, Xs.
John Bell, John Swynglehurst — Mentioned
Prayers for son of Alice, my wife.
John, son of John Bell
For a pilgrimage to Beverley and Bridlington, 2s.2d.
John, son of Richard, my son.
Richard, brother of the said John.
To 'fabricam novi pontis super Hodour juxta Slaytburn'—towards building new bridge over Hodder near Slaytburn—6s.8d.
Richard Alan of Roysden, William Clerke — Mentioned
To the building of the chapel of S. Leonard, 3s.
Residue to Robert, my son.
Executors : Robert, my son,
John Bell
John Swinglehurst.
Rector : Supervisor.
Witnesses : Thomas Richemond, Richard Mewton, John Ffranke — Chaplains.

Date : 1442—No day or month given till end of will. 22nd May.

HOLDEN. Margaret

Widow of Henry Holden.
Bur. in ch. of 'Slateburn'

Richard de Newton. chaplain.
William 'the clerk'
Richard Evyse & his wife unnamed.
Christine Proktour.
The daughter of John Langshaw.
Elizabeth Birche.
Alice Catlogh.
Margaret the daughter of Richard Badresby.
Sons of Robert my son.
Margaret my daughter.
Galfrid son of William Winkeley.
William Bolton.
Henry Cambe.
John the son of John Proktour.
Laurence the son of Robert Holden.
Ronald son of William Badresby.
John the son of Richard Evyse.
Robert Proktour.
Thomas my son.

Executor : Robert Holden.

STANDEN. Nicholas, of Slaidburne, Woodhouse in Bolland. Yeoman.

Date 14, March. 1636.

To Robert Standen 'which he was godfather to' a ewelamb or 4 shillings.
To Isabell his wife—half his sheep.
his brother William, mentioned
To Isabell his part of Covert in Ashton Close.
'Unkle William' mentioned.
Residue to Isabell and Executor. John Smythson. Richard Hairste.
Written by me William Smythson. Nicholas Standen.

WITTONN, JOHN Date: 27th April, 1638.

of Painehill in Bolland.

Jennett—my wife—to occupy, possess and enjoy Painehill.

Thomas Wittonn, John Wittonn, Elizabeth Wittonn, Margaret Wittonn } Children.

under care of Jenett until Thomas attains age of 21.
Robert Swinglehurste, Esquire to advise and councel Jenette.
Mr. Duckesbie
Edmund Rudd

Christopher Parkinson
Ffrancis Packett.

To be aydinge, assistinge and helpfull unto my said wife.
Henry Law of Heptonstall—executor.
John Woodward } Witnesses.
Thomas Mercer }

Date : 2nd March 1646-7

RICHMOND, HENRY. of the Stakes in Bolland—Gentleman.

Anne Richmond, Wife, all estate except legacies following.
To daughter Mary,—if she and husband perform articles agreed upon—that my wife to have profit and commodity of Stakes for two years,—to have the great Ark standing in the Kylchyne Chamber and six silver-spoons.
To my daughter's Son, Henry—1 of 3 Heiffers whichever my daughter chooses for him.
To my daughter the Jacke that is in the Kytchyne and one half of all husbandry gear, conditionally again on wife's being allowed to enjoy legacy peaceably.

TO : {
John Harrison.
Robert Marsden.
Edward Stubbs.
Thomas Alston.
Katheryne Deane.
Margaret Marshall.

20 mete of meal to be distributed among servants.[1]
Residue to Anne—Sole excutrix.

Witnesses : {
Christopher Hindley.
William Cundliffe.
William Tunneley.

PARKINSON, John — 4 March 1646
the elder of Brennand, husbandman

To Thomas P. his son all his messuage and farm at Brennand
Thomas must keep his mother or pay her £4
Elizabeth the mother to have the household goods
William his son £3
Agnes his daughter £3
To Thomas his son 20s. or the quantity of meal which John his son owes
To Robert Parkinson a housestead adjoining the farmhouse
Witness Robt Parkinson James Forest

[1] Mete is a dialect word for measure.

The Parkinsons were for centuries one of the clans of Bolland. Carved initials of the family still decorate Farrick and Sikes. At Farrick below the dovecote is the inscription : John Parkinson Dorothy his wife and Thomas his son, 1716. On the barn TDP

WP

1724

According to Miss Peel's *History of Slaidburn* these are on Birkett stone.

The Sikes inscriptions are AIP TMP IP 1692—the I is no doubt J

Date : 9th Sept. 1648.

HODGSON WILLIAM. husbandman of Stainemore in Bolland.

Bur. in Slaidburne churchyard.

To son John all lands—both freehold and copyhold except one half of freehold and copyhold—To Anne now said wife.

To son John all 'husbandrie geare' and loose boards in house.

Also—all my part of to my three daughters Janet, Alice and Elizabeth.

'Cowne' equally shared between four Children.

Elizabeth my daughter to have £30 two sheares and two twinters within one year after decease.

If not 2 acres of freehold lying or being in her hands until payment made.

Son John executor. Witnesses. John Bond John Standern.

Dunnow Hall is sited at Bottomley, a place named in the Domesday Book. The estate around the hall became known as Dunnow, replacing the earlier name. It was built by the King-Wilkinsons, another family whose history is so strongly linked with that of Bolland.

CHAPTER XXV.

HARROP.

NOTE BOOK OF MR. THOMAS OAKES WRIGHT.[1]

Gresford Bank, Gresford, Denbighshire.

1622/23 Duchy of Lancaster from the Book of Grants 20th James to Charles I in Somerset House. From the grant of James I to Edward Bradby and William Weltden, citizens of London in the 20th year of his reign for the sum of £2000, whose names are mentioned in the deeds of Harrop Hall and Nettel Carr estates.[2]

The Fee Farm Rents were sold by Edward Badby and William Weltden to the Duke of St. Alban's, and those of Harrop and Nettle Carr were sold by his descendant George Harley Drummond Esq. and his Trustees to Thomas Oakes on 12th April, 1811 for the sum of £118.6.8.

Harrop Hall—Mark Rents—in 8 parts I believe about 28 acres—Astleys—within Easington, lying so contiguous to Harrop Hall were purchased by my wife's father, for which he paid £700 is 25 acres. Mark Rents I find 38 a. 3 r. 32 p. including Oxengill Meadow and house, which is 9 a. 3 r. 25 p.—sold to W. King.

1783. An estate in Bolland near Harrop sold a little time before I purchased Harrop Hall for £2600 some odd besides paying £80 yearly rent which is not so valuable as Harrop Hall and the adjoining Farm, Langcliffe Cross—the latter farm is let to Henry Waddington for £25 a year. I had this information from Mr. Aspinall (Serjeaunt Aspinall's brother) who values land and who I paid for valuing Harrop Hall.

Langcliffe Cross Farm which was sold to Mr. King brought him a rent of £70 ann. in 1794.

In 1794 Nettle Carr let for £80 ann.

Newton Chapel built (as marked over door) by Mr. Leigh

---

16 96
R L

The Rev. Mr. Gillibrand left Newton Chapel in 1715.

Slaidburn Church dedicated to St. Andrew was built 1232.

Proved by Valor Ecclesiasticus in 26th Henry VIII wheat was then valued by the Commissioners at 6/8 a quarter, and at present 1815 at £6.13.4. Barley they value at 3/4. The ancient gallon measure was used.

[1] Printed by kind permission of his descendant, Professor C. Wright, and by the good offices of Messrs. Hatch, Solicitors, Wrexham.

[2] These farms were once the property of Whalley Abbey. Hence perhaps the name Cross for Nettley Carr. No trace of a cross remains.

In 1801 Far House in Grindleton was sold by T. Lister Parker, Esq., by public auction to Dr. St. Clair for about £2900 at the same time as I bought Parker Field for £150 which is tythe free.

Mowing Hay at the Heights above Harrop Lodge. The general time for mowing hay at Harrop, if the weather permits, is about 8 July. They do not leave off eating the grass intended for hay before 26 April in this neighbourhood on account of keeping the sheep upon the low lands until then.

Cross Copy is 24 acres and will take 2000 loads of lime besides draining.

1801 Game. The Rev. Henry Wigglesworth[1] says that his father killed by hunting in one season 97 brace of hares, and that he himself killed in one season by hunting upwards of 80 brace of hares.

1801 Oats now sold in this neighbourhood growing at 18 guineas an acre. In 1794 sold growing at Slaidburn £7 an acre.

It is estimated that Ellis Kay's corn on the Cross Estate is 70 bushells of the acre of 7 roods.

Oats July 24 1802. John Peels shot at Harrop Hall. Ellis Kays at Cross not shot, but the best corn in the country. It was sown late and this is the coldest season which has been known these many years.

In the year 1794 John Peel began shearing on the 29 August.

Imposition 1802. Paid for the land in the Forest for tithes until about 12 years past for Harrop Hall 12/4, for Nettle Carr (commonly called Cross) 7/4¾. This has been paid in latter times since Harrop Hall has been in the hands of Tenants and paid by them and others through ignorance. Not knowing that King James I had sold them from the Abbey of Whalley to Edward Badbie and Wm. Welden, which is regularly recorded in the deeds, and for which King James gave a regular grant and got an act of Parliament for so doing. See the grant in my possession. (Original grant in latin lies in the Duchy Court at Somerset House, London).

Harrop Hall estate contains customary measure 248 a. 0 r. 34 p.

1803 Land Tax. Paid for the Cross Estate £34-19-11½

1799 Land Tax Paid for Harrop Hall Estate £97-4-10½

Coolam Hall and Dean Slack estate contains 85 a. 0 r. 15 p.

Langcliffe Cross and Gauca Hills estate contains 80 a. 1 r. 9 p. sold to Mr. King for £1,100 including Oxengill meadow which did belong to Harrop Hall.

1804 12 July Harrop Hall and Cross Farm began mowing hay.

Baumers. Slater Dewhurst pays £48 a year for— He has more summer joist[2] than will pay his rent.

[1] Rector of Slaidburn.

[2] Agistment or pasturing of cattle for a fee.

Swallow Scars. T. Hanson pays £66 a year for, and lets the copy off to Todds of £30 per annum.

1805 Knowlmere Estate sold by the heirs of the late Turner Kerfoot to Jonathan Peel Esq. for £25,400.

L. Wilkinson received 7/4 a week for the Score of a house at Painhill.

In James Embley's bottom meadow the nearest to Harrop Folds are 63 trees—all in the hedge rows except one.

1805 August. Let Henry Hindle the Troughton Croft at £4.10.0 per annum.

Wheat. 1805 sold at £13 an acre growing on the Peel estate in Bolton parish.

A. N. Parker says he can let Heaning for 50/- an acre. It is about 80 acres.

Slaidburn Flatt. Mr. Parker of Browsholme lets to Robert Bleazard of Slaidburn for £168 per ann. It is 32 acres in one pasture.

1805 Let Harrop Hall to John and Christopher Dobson for £240 to expire 1816.

James Wiglesworth Esq. lived at Townhead.

1805 Oct. **Storth.** Messrs. Bates ask £15,000. Two years ago they gave £5,000 for it. Mr. Jonathan Peel and Mr. Taylor, surgeon of Heywood, are wishing to purchase it.[1]

Gauca Hill.

Harrop Hall. Messrs. Dobson charged Robert Chester 50/- for a summer's run for a cow.

Cross Farm. James Embley cleared last season £40 and upwards by taking in wintering goods. 140 sheep at 4/- ; 7 Galloways 24/- ; — Scots.

The whole neighbourhood have agreed for next season—sheep at 5/6 each.

1806. Spencers. William Brennand's estate is 27 acres.

John Pinder gamekeeper charges John Bolton Esq, 1/6 a week for the keep of each Pointer and his salary. He charges me as gamekeeper for Harrop 2/- a day and his meat. John Pinder had a farm of 11½ acres near Forest Becks and paid a rent of £40 a year for it.

Harrop and Nettle Carr.

Those parts which are in the Forest of Bolland are in the Chapelry of Whitewell which is within the Parish of Whalley. The farm house for Nettle Carr is within Grindleton in the Parish of Mytton.

[1] Storth is now a ruin, except farm buildings.

Parker Field Wall I agreed to give James Embley 8/- a rood for carting stone from the quarry and to pay Robert Chester for getting stone 6/- a rood and for the walling of ditto 2/6 a rood. It was 31 roods. New wall finished 1807.

Summering a cow 1806. They cannot summer one in the neighbourhood of Slaidburn for less than from £5 to £6. The keep of a cow for a year will cost from £10 to £12.

Slaidburn. There are in that village (what the Law calls) from ten to twelve qualified men. This shows that as a village consisting of Houses it is a very respectable and wealthy one.

Black Oats. John Dobson says Black Oats Straw is much better fodder than straw from white oats and when nearly ripe is not so apt to be shaken by the wind as the white,

Troughton Croft 1806. Josiah Cockshutt Twistleton's share of it, for which he had from time immemorial received 4/- a year rent for, was sold at the sale for £36 to Mr. John King, Attorney, Slaidburn, calling it 1/3 share of the Croft, the other 2/3 belonging to me.

Hay 1807. The general price of hay in Bolland has been the last spring at 15/- a yard. I Battersby paid John Simpson 14/6 per yard for some on my account.

1807 Harrop Hall. Messrs. Dobson have 30 Scots upon Broad Head this summer. They had 22 acres of corn last year. (On old map Broad Head is marked with note—once called Astleys.)

Cross Farm. James Embley's Scots, which he has in the copy, L. Wilkinson says should be upon the Fell and oxen in the copy, for Scots will not now pay to be kept there.

1807. My Meadow produced this year 14 loads of hay, large ones, besides the hay of the Moss. The meadow must have produced much more than ten tons.

Storth 1807. Mr. Peart of Settle has bought by auction for £8100. He has told Miss Wiglesworth the house is near down, and the money which has been laid out in Improvement has been thrown away, say £1000, for it is not better for it. I am at a loss to know his motive for saying this, for the House is not near down, and it is certainly improved.[1]

The Harrop Estates 1807 consisting of Harrop Hall and Nettle Carr, although they lie all within a ring fence except one field, are divided by the several townships of—The Forest of Bolland—Slaidburn—Easington and Grindleton (Grindleton is within the

[1] House must have been decayed as it is now a complete ruin.

parish of Mitton, which parish is part in Yorkshire and part in Lancashire). The boundary line of Craven runs nearly through the middle of the estate and divides Craven from the Forest of Bolland. The pews in the different place of worship are Whitewell in the Forest of Bolland—Slaidburn—Grindleton—and Newton, a Presbyterian chapel.

Those parts of the Harrop Hall and Nettle Carr estates which lie within the Forest are in the parish of Mitton, within the chapelry of Whitewell.

Ploughing Land on the Nettle Carr estate (James Embley was an unsatisfactory tenant, and behaved very ill in ploughing up much more than his agreement) and in 1808 he was given notice to leave the following spring.

Names of Fields. Slaidburn Field, Long Rigg, Barn Field, Ling Hill, Moss, Marles Heights, Rushy Field, Calf House Meadow.

10th of August 1808, Mr. Young at Bolton Hall began sheaving oats—an early white reddish oat, nearly the shape of the Black Oat and had the seed from Liverpool.

Sheep, etc., kept on the Nettle Carr estate 1808. Ellis Kaye when he farmed it kept upon it 70 to 80 head of cattle and James Embley has not above 30 head on it this summer. Neighbours say it is not half stocked, and I believe he has not above a score of sheep, but he takes a large stock for winter. Robert Turner used to keep a hundred sheep. Ellis Kaye kept about 60 sheep. Henry Simpson says if he takes the Cross (which he is anxious to do) he shall keep a 150 sheep.

W. Slack, a very well informed farmer upon Mr. Tomlin's estate near Dawford Bridge, says his cattle are very subject to Blackwater. He has much oak wood.

The charges of meat for workmen. By Messrs. Dobsons bill for meat for Paul Bond when repairing the cottage at Harrop Hall, they have charged 1/6 a day for his meat.

29 August 1808. Began shearing oats at Harrop Hall.

Robert Chester and Thurstan Tomlinson began 22 Aug. James Embley began shearing 1 Sept. (He ploughed for other people and sowed his oats late).

1808 Gradhill inshedding Lamb Hill, etc. Mr. Bramley has sold to Mr. Farrer of Clapham for upwards of £17,000. Mr. Bramley bought it for £9,000 and has had it for 10 years. He has improved it. It was sold by auction at Slaidburn.

Slaidburn Town Field. That part which is yet uninclosed is worth £100 an acre (of seven yards to the rood customary measure) says Mr. Tipping. In 1780 Mr. John Parker, attorney, Clitheroe, purchased grazes from the heirs of the late James Harrison, Esq. at £42 an acre in that Field uninclosed. Mr. Leonard Wilkinson has lately bought from T. L. Parker, Esq., Browsholme—acres uninclosed in the same Field at £— an acre. The price was left to Mr. W. Honor and knowledge of its value. This needs no comment.

1809 **Mr. Parker of Browsholme** advertised in the Lancaster paper to be sold by auction Nov. 29th at Robert Sutton's, the Bull Inn, Slaidburn, Bait Hall and Flatts in the possession of Robert Bleazard, whose term expires Spring 1811—containing about 50 acres at the yearly rent of £171. Rev. Henry Wiglesworth bought it for £6,000. Bait Hall is a house in Slaidburn and there is a barn in the field adjoining the churchyard.

Free Warren I have a grant of, from King James I, including royalties of all kinds, Court Leet, etc., besides tithes for Harrop Hall and Nettle Carr (commonly called Cross). Nettle Car is granted by that King to Edward Bradbie and William Welden of London by their Indenture of bargain and sale, under their hands 18th day of June, 22 year of James I and—Edward Parker Esq. of Browsholme, who are mentioned in the deeds for both estates.

1810 Storth Hall. Mr. Peart has sold Mr. Slater of Bradford part of the land from that estate, the low land at £60 an acre.

Harrop Hall estate contains of enclosed land 248 acres 34 perches customary of 7 yds. to the rood. Three acres of this measure being equal to five statute acres.

Nettle Carr Estate (commonly called Cross) contains of inclosed land 127 acres customary, besides the right of Harrop Fell and Broadhead Common.

1807 Witton Hills. Improved by stone and sod draining. 1284 loads of lime. Draining cost £87.7.4. Lime £48.3.0.

Mr. Wright quotes Rapin

"The Normans called them *Vavasors* and their lands *Vavasories*. Middle Thanes or 2nd class Thanes, and not many of them. Held their lands of the earls and barons.

1810 **Linneys,** an estate near Storth behind Newton which George Scott told me he received £63 a year for. Mr. Read is lately let for £205 a year. The last letting 9 years ago was for £110 a year.

1810. Mr. Wright was not living at Bolland but Knutsford.

1812. **Dunnow,** late Robert Parker's estate near Slaidburn is now let to John Frankland of Dean Slack at £320 a year. About

160 acres. See advertisement for selling 25th Feb. 1813. Mr. Leonard Wilkinson bought it for £11,000 or £11,500.

1815 **Harrop Hall,** let again to John and Cristopher Dobson who lived there with their mother Isabella Dobson for 7 years at a rent of £300. 248 acres. Large extent of common right.

Copy of letter sent to John and Cristopher Dobson, Harrop Hall, sent by Samuel Foden.

Messrs. Dobson, Liverpool, May 1812.

Gentlemen,

As I have purchased from Mr. Drummond the Fee Farm Rents of Near and Far Harrop, I think it is necessary to inform you, that in future you must pay them to Mr. Samuel Parker, who will receive them on my account, instead of paying them at Lancaster to Mr. Baxter (Mr. Drummond's agent), who has received them before, and inform the Farmers at Harrop that I hope they will pay Mr. S. Parker.

I have wrote a list of them below for that purpose. I am very much obliged for the Game you was so good to send me.

Gentlemen, Your Hble Serv.

Thomas Oakes.

Harrop Hall	19/-
John Mascar	6/8
Nettle Carr	14/4
Richard Bradley	13/4
Thurstan Charnley	11/8
Messrs. Alfred Kayley Harrop Folds	£2.15.0.

Liverpool, 28 August 1812.

Mr. William Silverwood, Jun.

Sir,

That there may be as little injury as possible to the crops and fences of the Nettle Carr and Harrop Hall Estates and that the Game may not be improperly destroyed, I hereby authorise you and Messrs. Dobsons at the Hall to order every person off the said estates to prevent intruders from killing game there save and except my friends Mr. Parker of Newton, the Rev. Mr. Wiglesworth, Townhead, Mr. L. Wilkinson, Slaidburn, and Mr. Bolton of Bolton, and such other persons as you may think proper.

Signed. Thomas Oakes.

Mr. William Silverwood Jun.

Harrop Lodge near Slaidburn,

Nov. 1812. Know Mere. J. Peel Esq. now talks of selling and ask £40,000. He paid in 1805 £25,000, but has improved it by fencing and draining.

29 April 1816 William Silverwood Senr. came for the two leases for Harrop Lodge and the Cross Farm to prove the rent of each estate for the satisfaction of the Income Tax Commissioners.

My 29 1816 Hay in Bolland. William Silverwood Senr. says it sells in the neighbourhood of Settle 15/- a yard but in his district it is only worth about 10/-.

July 1817 **Harrop Folds** more properly Far Harrop, Harrop Hall is Near Harrop. There has lately been sold 12 acres. There is a good house. It is part of the late Richard Bradley's estate.

Copy of leave for shooting. I hereby authorise Anthony Littledale Esq. to shoot upon Harrop Fell. Witness my hand 22 Aug. 1818.

Liverpool. Thomas Oakes.

Yorkshire Note Book of the late Thomas Oakes Esq., of Harrop Hall, Yorks. Died 22 Aug. 1819 aged 64 years.

Smelfthwaites, Newton, is a typical Bolland farmhouse. Its origins go back several centuries, and it is seen here in the 1930s. The portion on the left was built at a different period to the rest of the house, which has a granary built on to the top end. It has a vegetable garden and an orchard enclosed by stone walls.

Haymaking in the 1930s. The Frankland family farmed Smelfthwaites, Newton, with the help every year of some Irish labourers who went from farm to farm. Their raking done, the hay is about to be dragged on a sledge to the barn. Meanwhile three of the labour force are enjoying the *baggin'* brought out to them by Mrs Frankland.

INDEX OF BOLLAND PLACES.

ACKNOWLEDGMENTS.

The authors are grateful to the many farmers in Bolland and beyond who helped them in their numerous enquiries. They retain happy memories of numerous encounters with the farming population which would not have taken place except for the writing of this book.

Colonel Robert Parker, of Browsholme, befriended our plan from the beginning and most graciously entrusted to us any of his father's notes that he could find.

Lord Assheton, of Clitheroe, very kindly allowed us free access to the ancient documents belonging to the Honor of Clitheroe, preserved in Clitheroe Castle. At the castle the authors were received with unfailing courtesy and every assistance by Colonel N. Robinson.

We are also indebted to His Honour Judge Robert Peel, of Knollmere, for the loan of Miss Peel's privately printed history.

Colonel and Mrs. L. King-Wilkinson were always most willing to help us in the Slaidburn area, and took us on a memorable visit to Hamerton Hall.

Captain Frank Mitchell, of Clitheroe, has been a useful and discriminating helper. Tramping the hills with him has always been one of the joys of our quest.

Index to Surnames, with Associated Places

LIST OF SUBSCRIBERS

Michael P Conroy, Tottington
Michael Holden, Lewes
Denise Conchar, Bingley
Jennifer S Holt, Haslingden
Mrs Caroline Warner, Garforth
Ronald Webb, Galashiels
Barbara Palmer, Ramsbottom
Gillian Ryall, Newbridge, Gwent
Muriel Charnley, Rathmell
Edward Huddleston, Bentham
Jean M Bell, Hexham
John Lambert, Clitheroe
John Buckley, Torrisholme
Peter Foley, Holden Clough Nursery, Holden
Peter and Mary Cowking, Pages Farm, Slaidburn
E & M C Higham, Clitheroe
Mrs Anne Newton, Back Lane, Slaidburn
Douglas Wilson, Todmorden
T O Roberts, Settle
Jane King-Wilkinson, Bruton, Somerset
Thomas Woodcock, Whiteholme, Slaidburn
Mrs Andrew Penny, Ribchester
Mr & Mrs John Tomlinson, Stratford-on-Avon
Michael Slinger, Saffron Walden
John B Richardson, Ormskirk
Bill Harrison, Giggleswick
Dorothy Taylor, Waddington
D Lawson, Clitheroe
Mark Etheridge, Cardiff
Faith W Finegan, Settle
Christopher Swindlehurst, Keighley
Alan Parkinson, Blackpool
May Jackson, Clitheroe
Margaret Clough, Atherton
Marsden family, West Bradford
Jen and Brian Sanders, Chaigley
Paul and Pauline Bywood, Clitheroe
David and Julia Bain, Lytham St Annes
Deborah Knight, South Croydon
Carrie Dugdale, Lytham St Annes
Brennands Endowed Primary School, Slaidburn
Mrs J Lawson, Chapel St, Slaidburn
Mrs J Frankland, Gisburn
Rita Holden, Blackburn
Frank Robinson, Harrop Fold.
Mrs Marion Fox, Clitheroe
Patrick J Clews, Leeming, Australia
Muriel Humphries, Burton in Lonsdale
Thomas and Cecilia Croston, Bolton-by-Bowland
Irena Preston, Chipping
Rod J Ireland, Leyland
Cliff Astin, Clayton-le-Moors
Roger Butler, Bromley
Roy Preston, Whitworth
Mrs Barbara H Smith, Wiswell
M M Shaw, Lower Highfield, Slaidburn
Edith Davy, Mellor
Mrs Dorothy Faraday, Bentham
Russell Ingham, New Zealand
Meriwether Cowgill Schmid, Connecticut
David and Gillian Cowking, Langshaw Farm, Slaidburn
Brian Walker Townend, Slaidburn
Bolton-By-Bowland C of E Primary School
Rex Pope, Brabbin's House, Newton in Bowland
Val Martin-Warren, Longridge
Derek Hicks, Longridge
Paul Holden, Blackburn
Clitheroe Royal Grammar School
Vera Newhouse, Tosside
Mrs Patricia Bennett, Thorneyholme
Vincent Gee, Walkden
Shirley Herbert, Elstree
Shirley Anne Robson, Farington
Miss Maureen E Smith, Nelson
J F C and H M Parry, Lower Stony Bank, Slaidburn
Mrs Meg Lawson, Clitheroe
Mrs Winifred Fox, Ivy Cottage, Dunsop Bridge
Mrs Tracey Pinder, Chapel Street, Slaidburn
Bro. John-Paul Sanderson O.C.S.O., Mount St Bernard Abbey
John Thomas Brennand, Clitheroe
Fred Peel, Clitheroe
Mrs H M Taylor, Clitheroe
John H Whitehead, Clitheroe
Mrs Beatrice Townson, Clitheroe
Roger Nicholas Thomas, Harborne, Birmingham
Tony Goodbody, Clitheroe

Krystyna Taylor, Chipping
Mrs Muriel Leeming, Bromborough
Mrs Vera Eccles, Bishops House, Dunsop Bridge
Kathleen M Metcalfe, Clitheroe
Philip and Maud Elgey, Clayton-le-Moors
Bruce and Marian Kitchin, Blackburn
Mrs J M Brooks, Clitheroe
Jean Faulkner, Bristol
Peter Llewellyn, Clitheroe
Margaret Holden, Clitheroe
John N King-Wilkinson, The Brooklets, Slaidburn
John Trotter, Clitheroe
David and Pauline Paterson, Chipping
Christine M Haworth, Barrowford
Mrs M Parr, Clitheroe
Miss Hazel Addison, Accrington
Ben and Margaret Edwards, Preston
H M Kenyon, Ribchester
Mr and Mrs Frank Rickitt, Durham
Ian Driver, Clitheroe
Jason Dalton, Lancaster
Christoper Parker, Browsholme Hall
Connor James Loebell, Clitheroe
Michael G Leigh, Barnoldswick
Sheila Brennand Shaw, Mellor
Gordon Taylor, Clitheroe
Richard Bowman, The Inn at Whitewell
Leo Warren, Accrington
Stanley Rushton, Clitheroe
C E Scruff Hargreaves, Olney
Mr & Mrs L Tunney, Burnley
Kenneth Porter, Huddersfield
Geoff Taylor, Accrington
Jean Till, Accrington
Winifred McClelland, Clitheroe
T I Roberts, Sheffield
James Peter Curwen, Abbeystead
Michael Keith Curwen, Abbeystead
George Duckworth, Rishton
Kenneth William Range, Garstang
Gordon Hartley, Burnley
Roy Pearson , Boston, Lincs
Mrs Deidre Robinson, Dean Slack Farm, Slaidburn
Mr and Mrs G A Wilkinson, Chipping
The Littlefair family, Slaidburn
Margaret Hocking, Chew Magna, Somerset
Marie Messenger, Ben Rhydding
Robert S Edelston, Longridge
Judith Turner, Brisbane
Harold Owen, Oswaldtwistle
Stuart & Gay Crook, Northwich
Lily Roberts, Blackburn
Dorothy Thomas, Church
Roger Gifford, London
John P Lynch, Oswaldtwistle
Geoff Garnett, Oswaldtwistle
Miss Helen E Holdsworth, Accrington
Heather Jenkinson, Blackburn
Dr Frank Dewhurst, Leicester
Andrew Dewhurst, Arnside
Peter Worden, Blackburn
Tony Norris, Bromley
Dr Rosemary Jenkins, Clapham
Roman Cizdyn, Lancaster
Craig Thornber, Macclesfield
Wm. Worthington, Penwortham
Donald Mellor, Keighley
Thomas G Hargreaves, Calgary
Ivan James King, Clitheroe
J & G Blanc, Clitheroe
Roger Prestwich, Elland
Mr and Mrs Harold Douglas Brennand, New Orleans
Allison Brennand George, Houston, Texas
Ann Brennand Watson, San Antonio, Texas
Marion Ormerod, Accrington
Brian and Joyce Jackson, Penwortham
Barry & Jan Marsden, Skelshaw Farm, Newton In Bowland
Allan & Jackie Clements, Bolton By Bowland,
Rob Veitch, Sawley
Roy S Hilton, Wymeswold
Mrs C Lawson, Clitheroe
Sam Herron, Brighouse
Jane Lewis, Hare & Hounds Barn, Newton in Bowland
Lewis Family, Hare & Hounds Barn, Newton in Bowland
Lorna M Webb, Clitheroe
Anne & Keith Richards, Harrogate
Jim Wrathall, Garstang
Barry M Hunt, Nelson
Mrs Jennie Wilkinson, Church Gates, Bolton-By-Bowland
Mrs Brenda Kay, Clitheroe
Mrs Elizabeth Harrison, Colne
Thomas Houghton, Billington
Ronald King, Clitheroe
University of Central Lancashire Library, Preston
Doreen Ainscough, Eastbourne
Alan W Waterworth, Kingsley, Cheshire
Lawrence Haworth, Woking
Phil Marsden, New Ash Green, Kent
Brian & Christine Crumblehulme, Bolton
Jacqueline Quarmby, Guisborough
Mr and Mrs F S Dinsdale, Alder House, Bolton-By-Bowland
Barbara Kitchin, Chipping
Diane Waters, Orpington
Margaret Brenchley, Bracknell

Tom Latto, Southport
Thomas Wroe, Micklehurst
Mrs E Waterworth, Shay House Farm, Slaidburn
Bruce Houlker, Clitheroe
Lancaster University Library
John Payne, Caton
Gordon Christie, Barrow in Furness
Malcolm Jones, Culvert Cottage, Newton-in-Furness
Bill Bowker, Chipping
John Watson, W. Australia
PC Michael Horne, Dolphinholme
Margaret Smith, Poulton-le-Fylde
Dr Brenda Fox, Garstang
Gill & Rebekah Fox, Oakworth
Peter Rawling, Bracknell
John Coates, Clitheroe
Jenny & Donald Bradley, Clitheroe
Ronnie Webster, Whalley
Colin V Redmayne, Accrington
Fred Sedgwick, Clitheroe
John Preston, Lowestoft
Brian Dugdale, West Bradford
Anthony Petyt, Wakefield
Dr Garry Lord, Loughborough
Ted Metcalfe, Barrow-in-Furness
Audrey Cooper, Haslingden
Carl Haythornthwaite, Broughton-in-Furness
John Michael Turner, St Annes on Sea
Peter K Hawthornthwaite, Leicester
Anthony David Hall, Cheadle Hulme
Marie Celine Craven, Carlisle
Ron Brierley, Bolton
Carole A Walker, Penwortham
Norah Gilbert nee Bowland, Scarborough
Rev David Lannon, Burnley
Nick Cansfield, Wokingham
Joan Hamilton, New Zealand
Mrs Marie Ashworth, Chorley
Mrs Sylvia Brown, Chorley
Ian Whittaker, Pontefract
Mrs Kathleen Taylor, Phynis Farm, Slaidburn
Rex Watson, Cambridge
Mrs M Cartright, Hurst Green
Howard Hammersley, Ashton on Ribble
Richard Ewart Rawstron, New Zealand
Mrs Jenny Childs, Market Harborough
Roy & Christine Cross, Broughton
Richard Slinger, Rudloe, Wilts
Margaret Mary Glynn, Disley
Barbara Gill, Colchester
Harriette Shaw, Lower Birkett, Newton In Bolland
Bloynan, Lower Birkett, Newton In Bolland
Maureen Shakeshaft, St Annes on Sea
Mr & Mrs D Higham, Hillcrest Cottage, Slaidburn
Joy Leslie, nee Seed, Pickering
Susan Ellis, Newchurch in Rossendale
Norman & Ingrid Hollinghurst, Longridge
David Fisher, Clitheroe
Norman Barnard Witham, Barnt Green, Worcs.
Chris & Linda Smith, Penwortham
Jean Cuthbertson, Brookhouse
Evelyn & James Whittaker, Heysham
Mrs Margaret Frances Lupton, Witney
Nick Howorth, Brampton
David Hollings, Rimington
Ian Cucknell, Guildford
Dorothy Ashburn Canham, Leyland
Anthony Owen, Bolton
E F Greenwood, Wirral
John Robert Bond, Lancaster
Mr & Mrs S Wallbank, Halsteads Farm, Slaidburn
Stephen Wood, Chapel House, Slaidburn
Roy Gudgeon, Lawkland
Mary Newborne, High Wycombe
Lucy Day, Barton
Len Middleton, Whalley
Tom Codling, Great Harwood
Mollie Hood, Clitheroe
Sir Mark Lennox-Boyd, Caton
Mrs Joan B. Sharman, Coleford
Father John Chaloner, Dunsop Bridge
Mrs Joan Barber, Ontario
Mrs Monica Cowking, Lower Copy Nook
Bessie Lomas B.Ed (Hons), Baxenden
Elizabeth Pearson, Hothersall
Richard David Thomson, Fulwood
Mrs Cherrie R Johannesen, British Columbia
Mrs Barbara Lawson, Waddington
Donald R. Cundall , Pennsylvania
John Bailey, Billington
Janice Tolson, Clitheroe
J R Williams, Fulwood
Nichola Eastwood, Newton-in-Bowland
Raymond McNair, Crumpsall
Mr & Mrs E Walmsley, Holden
Mrs Linda Reich, Dannstadt, Germany
John Holden, Burnley
Michael & Mary Lord, Accrington
Barry & Shirley Singleton, Dunsop Trout Farm
Andrew & Hilda Johnson, Thornton-Cleveleys
Richard Henry Tedstone, Dunsop Trout Farm
Richard Fleetwood Tedstone, Weegena, Tasmania
Allen Hollingworth, Rimington
Roger Atkinson, Chester

July 2000.